Raising pre-teens?

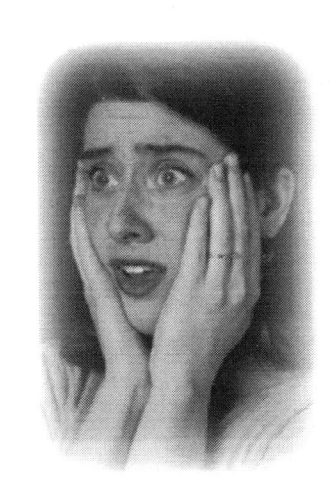

Don't Freak…..

Tweak……

and EMPOWER Them for Life!

An INTERACTIVE, LIFE LESSONS WORKBOOK for parents, concerned others, and their pre-teens that will SHAPE THEIR LIVES and prepare them for HEALTHY RELATIONSHIPS!

Tom Kidd ME-PD

Copyright 2014

Thomas F. Kidd

The material in this book is informational, intended to enlighten and inspire parents and their pre-teens. The information is not so much intended to replace the reader's present parenting skills as to improve and augment those skills. Any application of the information and interactive activities in this book are at the discretion of the reader who is solely responsible for their use and application. The author understandably assumes no responsibility for parenting actions taken by the reader since they are beyond his knowledge or control.

All rights are reserved. No part of chapters 1-11 may be reproduced by any mechanical, photographic, or electronic process or any form of audio recording; nor may it be stored in a retrieval system, transmitted, or otherwise be copied for public or private use without prior written permission of the author, other than "fair use" as brief quotations. Of course the interactive activities #1-12 are intended to be copied for personal use but may not be altered and reproduced for distribution without prior written permission of the author.

Cover and chapter photography by **Smmgphotography Photography LLC**,
Sarah Genskow
Editing and formatting by Mr. Jim Rapp
Occasional clip art by Microsoft Office

ISBN 13: 978-1496193216

Foreword
Dr. Dick Detert

I have read Tom Kidd's book, cover to cover, and found it to be an excellent tool for parents of pre-teens to discuss important health issues with them. This interactive book can be educational for both parents and their pre-teen, with an emphasis on developing effective communication. Parents have the opportunity to select important health topics based on comfort level and need. Discover a plethora of information on health issues that your pre-teen will encounter and assist them in making healthy choices as you navigate these years together. I highly recommend this book for both parents and their pre-teens.

Acknowledgements

Special thanks to the following for their preview and review of this book:

1. Dr. Richard Detert, Ph. D (Health and Wellness Promotion Professor – University of Wisconsin-La Crosse)
2. Ms. Stephanie Rowe (Health Educator – Wisconsin Public School System)
3. Mr. and Mrs. Geno and Katie Skudlarczyk (parents)
4. Mr. and Mrs. Dan and Christi Slowey (parents, teacher and principal)

Their expertise in the previewing of this teen-parent workbook was priceless. Not only are they true professionals, but I can call them true friends. Special thanks to a former colleague and friend, Mr. Jim Rapp, who kindly agreed to edit and format the book. Sincere thanks, as well, to my wife Deb. Her support, patience, understanding and encouragement while parenting and while I wrote the book are extremely appreciated. Watching our children CJ and Katelyn grow and develop was a blessing, a real education and an inspiration to write this book. The many experiences we encountered while parenting, and my interactions with pre-teens for over 30 years in my health education classroom, has equipped me to write this interactive guide.

Preface

Between the ages of 12-22, your children have been or soon will be faced with many critical decisions in their lives. It is important for you to understand what you can do to prepare them for those impending decisions. Keeping the communication lines open from a very young age is vitally important, creating the foundation upon which to build a well-rounded healthy teenage life. This book will not only make you aware of what you need to do to empower your pre-teens but also provides specific activities that will open the door of communication between you and them. Once that door is open and trust is built, a safer and more nurturing discussion will take place regarding life-altering decisions they will eventually have to make on their own. The knowledge you gain from this book and the experiences you have when talking with, AND listening to, your pre-teens will dramatically increase the opportunities for your children to have a life of health, happiness and success. Enjoy becoming a better parent than you already are!

Introduction

Congratulations! The mere fact that you are reading this book demonstrates the love, care and concern you have for your children. Parenting is not easy today. You are to be commended for reaching out to secure available and accurate resources to assist you in your demanding job.

As a parent, classroom educator for thirty-two years, and now a grandparent, I share your many concerns, apprehensions, wishes and dreams for today's adolescents. As our children enter the chapter in their life called "teen years," we try our hardest to divert them from the many dangers that life has to offer. This decision-making chapter of their lives is an enormously critical one and could change the way they live for their entire lifetime. We are constantly looking for information, for answers – for the how-to's – that enable us to set the stage for our children's lives. Parents often speak lightly about "loosening the apron strings," when to give them the "sex talk," or when to let them begin to make their own decisions; but as the time to do those things draws near they are no longer light matters.

Years of parenting and teaching health education convinces me that we need to intentionally develop empowered teens by giving them the needed knowledge, assets and life skills that will guide them to healthy, happy and successful lives. I also believe parental guidance is an on-going process until our children leave the family nest and often a long time afterwards. Critical life decisions like alcohol use, drug use, sexual activity and relationships all have to be anticipated and discussed before the pre-teen or teenager is exposed to them. I believe the time to address these issues is when they are in their tweener or pre-teen years, from ages 11-14.

The first nine chapters of this book will raise your awareness of the hazards facing pre-teens and teenagers. The remainder of the book provides activities you can use with your pre-teen to help them gain the knowledge and life skills to become an empowered young person.

Several studies have concluded that the portion of a teen's brain (the pre-frontal cortex) that is responsible for moral reasoning and looking ahead at consequences doesn't physically develop until they are about 21 years of age, long after the teen years! So, I have developed cooperative exercises that will intentionally and consciously get your pre-teens to consider their impending choices ahead of time so that their big decisions in life won't be impaired by alcohol, drugs and or hormones. They will learn to act in a pro-active manner instead of yielding to the intense pressures from their peers and our media.

This book is intended to be shared with your pre-teen. So enjoy reading, learning, building trust and growing with your children as you use this interactive parent/pre-teen workbook. It will assist you as you nurture and prepare them to enjoy healthy lifestyles and meaningful relationships.

I've kept the chapters brief because I understand you are busy raising children. However, chapters 1-10 are packed with useful information you can use when working with your pre-teen on the related interactive activities located at the end of the book. You will find yourself revisiting them to glean information you and your pre-teen need to complete the exercises and interactive activities.

Some clarifications right up front:

1. In the pages that follow I will refer to the child you will be working with as a "pre-teen." Pre-teens are children ages 11-14. Some of the information in this book you may deem to be very appropriate to share with your pre-teen; some you may not. As parents, you decide if the material is age-appropriate for your pre-teen. I tend to believe that earlier is better.

2. I, by no means, claim to have been a perfect parent. I learned from my mistakes at times, as we all do, and employed repeatedly the things that worked. But, in working with parents and pre-teens for more than 30 years, I have gleaned many strategies that are critical and many things that have been proven to work with this age group.

3. If, by chance, you are reading this book and your child is a teen already (ages 15-18), most, if not all, of the interactive activities are still appropriate and would be recommended for use. "It's never too late!"

4. When I use the term "parent," I am including categories such as the child's caretaker, guardian, mentor, teacher, etc. So basically, when using the word "parent" I am referring to anyone who cares enough to work with the pre-teen.

5. When I use the term "relationships," typically I would be referring to opposite sex relationships. But, as we know, this is not the situation all of the time. So when the word is used, it is in regards to *any two (or more) people* wanting a healthy relationship.

Contents

Foreword iii
Acknowledgements v
Preface vii
Introduction ix
Chapter 1: Why It Is Critical To Communicate With Your Pre-teen 1
Chapter 2: General Parenting Suggestions to "Set The Stage" 23
Chapter 3: You Say, When? Where? How? Why? 29
Chapter 4: What Makes Teens Successful 31
Chapter 5: Empowering Your Pre-teen with Goals, Dreams, and Wishes 39
Chapter 6: Understanding Healthy and Unhealthy Teen Relationships 43
Chapter 7: Understanding the Sexual Relationship Continuum 47
Chapter 8: The Many Consequences of Teenage Sexual Activity 51
Chapter 9: Critical Life Skills Your Pre-teen Needs to Know and Utilize 55
Chapter 10: Keys to Dating and Experiencing Healthy Relationships 67
Chapter 11: Let's Work Together – Time to Interact 71
Conclusion 73
Interactive Activity #1: Definitions Missing 75
Interactive Activity #2: Assessing My Assets 77
Interactive Activity #3: Life Decisions with Impact 89
Interactive Activity #4: Goals, Wishes and Dreams 93
Interactive Activity #5: Creating Healthy Teen Relationships 101
Interactive Activity #6: Consequences, Consequences, Consequences 103
Interactive Activity #7: Hormones Out of Control 107
Interactive Activity #8: Pros and Cons of Abstinence 111
Interactive Activity #9: Life Skills – My Toolbox for Life 113
Interactive Activity #10: Am I Ready? 123
Interactive Activity #11: Mutual Expectations 127
Interactive Activity #12: Pre-teen and Parent Contract to Live Well 131
Readings for Parents 133

YAKITY-YAK

Chapter 1

Why it is Critical to Communicate with Your Pre-teen

When you don't communicate with your child, you *have communicated* with your child. Your silence sends a message which your child may interpret in several ways: 1) my parents don't love me, 2) my parents care about other people, activities, or things more than they care about me, 3) my parents don't care what I do, 4) my parents will not know what I'm doing.

The most important component of successful parenting is open communication. Your child needs to know that he or she can come to you with any concern and feel comfortable discussing it with you. The youngest child in your household should receive the same respect and honesty when discussing their concerns that you would give to any adult.

Learning to communicate with your pre-teen takes time, trust and a lot of work. You will learn, in this book, some of the keys to effective communication: waiting for the child to speak his or her mind without prodding, listening without judging, and not being afraid to tell your child, "I don't know," just to name a few. It is sometimes difficult communicating with pre-teens and teenagers when they project the attitude that adults know absolutely nothing. I'll be sharing three life skills later in the workbook that will prepare you for those vexing conversations. Those life skills include a communication skill, an active listening skill and the Care-frontation skill.

For now, you need to realize that raising children well, in today's environment, is one very tough job. As I travel the U.S., providing trainings and sharing my presentations, my goal is to make available to those in attendance, the insights acquired while employed in my two jobs: full-time parent and health educator, speaker and trainer.

The enormously influential media relentlessly bombards our children with sexually-laden messages, scenes of instant gratification, and explicit approval of self-destructive behaviors presented as though they were the norm. Soon your children will be making life-determining decisions that will directly impact their present lives and their future potential. It is imperative that parents know the scope of the challenges facing adolescents today. It is just as important to use that knowledge to prevent them from getting caught in a "web of destruction."

I want to share some facts with you that may be alarming, but will also increase your awareness of the world that teenagers enter when they leave the safety of your home, school, church, etc. Knowledge is power. Your first step in communicating well with your child is to arm yourself with facts. Although the following facts are stark and may be grim, my purpose is to clearly demonstrate an urgent need to communicate and implement prevention strategies with your pre-teen.

Feel free to peruse and highlight the facts and statistics you may want to have readily available for your discussion with your pre-teen.

Facts about Alcohol and drugs:

Here are some things you should know:

- One of five seventh graders experience two or more problems caused by drinking alcohol. (A school problem is frequently one of them.)
- Two of three teenage pregnancies are alcohol or drug related.
- One of four children live in a home with a parent or set of parents who have an alcohol problem.
- Children of alcoholics are four to five times more likely to become alcoholics themselves.
- More than half of the teens who try marijuana for the first time are regularly using it one year later.
- More teenagers use marijuana than smoke cigarettes.

Here are some additional facts:

- Alcohol use by persons under the age of 21 is a major public health problem.[1]
- Alcohol is the most commonly used and abused drug among youth in the U.S., more than tobacco and illicit drugs, and is responsible for the death of more than 4,300 underage youths annually.[2]
- A nationwide survey showed that 20.5 percent of students have drunk alcohol (other than a few sips) before age 13. (That is 1 of 5).[3]
- In a nationwide survey 21.9 percent of students reported consuming five or more drinks of alcohol within two hours on at least one day in the month before the survey. In other words, one in five engaged in binge drinking.[3]
- Nationwide, 8.1 percent of students have tried marijuana before age 13.[3]
- Nationwide, 23.1 percent of students admitted using marijuana one or more times during the month before the survey.[3]
- In 2013, seven percent of eighth graders, 18 percent of tenth graders and 22.7 percent of twelfth graders reported using marijuana in the last month, up from 5.8 percent, 13.8 percent and 19.4 percent respectively in 2008.[4]
- Synthetic marijuana, also known as Spice or K2, was used by 11.4 percent of high school seniors in the past year.[4]

- Marijuana has a chemical in it called 9-tetrahydrocannibinol, better known as THC, along with approximately 400 other chemicals. In the 60s and 70s the THC content of marijuana was 6 – 7 percent. Today most marijuana used has at least 10 percent THC.[5]

---

1. U.S. Department of Health and Human Services. *The Surgeon General's Call to Action to Prevent and Reduce Underage Drinking.* Rockville, MD: U.S. Department of Health and Human Services; 2007.
2. Centers for Disease Control and Prevention (CDC). Alcohol-Related Disease Impact (ARDI). Atlanta, GA:CDC.
3. Youth Risk Behavior Surveillance. *Morbidity and Mortality Weekly Report.* June 8th, 2012. Vol. 61. No. 4.
4. National Institute on Drug Abuse-*Monitoring the Future* survey, 2013 report.
5. National Institute on Drug Abuse. Drug Facts: Marijuana (http://www.drugabuse.gov/publications/drug facts/marijuana). Bethesda, MD. NIDA, NIH, DHHS. Revised December 2013. Retrieved November 2013.

Facts about Prescription Drug Abuse:

Here are some things you should know:

- Teenage use and misuse of prescription drugs has increased by one third since 2008.
- Nearly one third of parents believe stimulants can improve academic performance.
- The majority of teenagers obtain their drugs from their parent's liquor supply and prescription drug cabinets.

Here are some additional facts:

- One in four teens (24 percent) reports having misused or abused a prescription drug at least once in their lifetime (up from 18 percent in 2008 to 24 percent in 2012), which translates to about five million teens.[1]
- Of those youths who said they abused Rx medications, one in five (20 percent) had done so before the age of 14.[1]
- One-third of teens (33 percent) say they believe it is okay to use prescription drugs that were not prescribed for them to deal with injury, illness or physical pain.[1]
- One in eight teens (about 2.7 million) now reports having misused or abused the drug Ritalin, or Adderall,[*] at least once in their lifetime.[1]
- One in four teens (26 percent) believes that prescription drugs can be used as a study aid.[1]

---

[1] The Partnership at Drugfree.org; MetLife Foundation. The Partnership Attitude Tracking Study (PATS) 2008-2012 Cassie Goldberg. April, 2013.

[*] These drugs are commonly prescribed for ADD (Attention Deficit Disorder) or ADHD (Attention Deficit Hyperactive Disorder).

Facts about Teenage Depression/Suicide:

Here are some things you should know:

- In the U.S., a teen suicide occurs at the rate of one every ninety minutes.
- Half of teens who successfully commited suicide were under the influence of drugs or alcohol.
- Most depression among teenagers stems from school-related issues.
- Teens often choose to use drugs, alcohol and/or sexual activity to cope with depression.
- Self- injury (or cutting – a process of teens intentionally cutting, burning or hurting themselves) is a destructive strategy teens often engage in when depressed.

Here are some additional facts:

- About 20 percent (1 of 5) of teens will experience depression before they reach adulthood.
- Between 10 –15 percent of teens have symptoms of depression at any given time.
- Teenage boys are less likely to seek help for their depression.
- Thirty percent of teens with depression also develop a substance abuse problem.
- Depressed teens are more likely to have trouble at school and in jobs, and struggle with relationships.

Statistics resources:

1. Mental Health: A Report of the Surgeon General. (online)
2. Kidshealth.org from the Nemours Foundation, "Understanding Depression." (online)
3. Center for Mental Health Services, SAMHSA, A Family Guide, Keeping Youth Mentally Healthy and Drug Free, "Depression Hurts." (online)
4. U.S. National Library of Medicine and National Institutes of Health, Medline Plus Medical Encyclopedia, "Depression Signs in Teenagers." (online)
5. Mental Health: A Report of the Surgeon General, "Depression and Suicide in Children and Adolescents." (online)
6. WebMD.com : Depression in Childhood Adolescence. (online)
7. WebMD/The Cleveland Clinic "Seasonal Depression." (online)

Facts about Bullying and Cyber-bullying:

Here are some things you should know:

- Cyber-bullying can be more dangerous than verbal or physical bullying since it often is anonymous or purports to come from another known person or group of people.
- Revenge for bullying is one of the most frequent motivations for school shootings.
- If our youth were taught, through appropriate modeling, to be empathetic, we'd have less bullying.

Here are some additional facts:

- In a nationwide survey, 20.1 percent of students reported being bullied on school property during the previous twelve months. [1]
- Most bullying occurs in grades four through eight, with 90 percent of students claiming to have been the victim of some kind of bullying. [2]
- Fifty-six percent of students say they have witnessed a bullying incident at school. [2]
- Fifteen percent of students say they have failed to show up for school out of fear of being bullied. [2]
- Seventy-one percent of students report that bullying is an ongoing problem. [2]
- Over 50 percent of adolescents and teens have been bullied online, and about the same number have engaged in cyber-bullying. [2]
- More than one in three young people have experienced cyber threats online. [2]
- Over 25 percent of adolescents and teens have been bullied repeatedly via cell phones or the internet. [2]
- More than 50 percent of young people do not tell their parents when cyber-bullying occurs. [2]

---

1. Youth Risk Behavior Surveillance. *Morbidity and Mortality Weekly Report.* June 8th, 2012. Vol. 61. No. 4.
2. makebeatsnotbeatdowns.org, olweus.org .

Facts about Sexual Activity:

Here are some things you should know:

- Fifty percent of teens never talk to their parents about sex-related issues.
- Most teenagers have an exaggerated opinion of how sexually active their peers are.
- Nine out of ten teenagers say that "being in love" makes premarital sex okay – two of three teenagers claim to have been "in love."
- Few teenage girls planned to engage in their first sexual intercourse – alcohol, hormones or drugs induced them to engage in sex.

When more than one significant person in a young person's life regularly and consistently talk to them about sexual issues it greatly reduces the chances for early teenage sexual activity!

Here are some additional facts:

- In a national survey, 47.4 percent of students reported having sexual intercourse. [1]
- In the same survey, 15.3 percent reported having had sexual intercourse with four or more persons. [1]
- Over six percent had their first sexual intercourse before age 13. (Nine percent for male and 3.4 percent for female.) [1]
- Thirty-three percent of those surveyed nationally reported having had sexual intercourse with at least one person during the three months prior to the survey. [1]
- Sexual relationships between young teens and older partners are more likely to involve risky sexual behaviors. [2]
- Five percent of 12 year-olds, 10 percent of 13 year-olds, and 20 percent of 14 year-olds are sexually active. [3]
- More than a quarter of sexually active 12- to 14-year-olds reported having multiple partners in the past 18 months. [4]
- Twelve percent of 12- to 14-year-olds involved in a "romantic relationship" are dating someone three years or more older than themselves. [5]
- Sexually-active teens are six times more likely to drink, five times more likely to smoke, and four times more likely to try marijuana than virgins. [6]

1. Youth Risk Behavior Surveillance. *Morbidity and Mortality Weekly Report.* June 8th, 2012. Vol. 61. No. 4.
2. Haydon, A.A. & Halpern, C.T. (2010). Older romantic partners and depressive symptoms during adolescence. *Journal of Youth and Adolescence*, 39 (10), 1240-1251.
3. Albert, B., Brown, S., & Flannigan, C. (Eds.) (2003), 14 and Younger: The Sexual Behavior of Young Adolescents Summary), Washington DC: National Campaign to Prevent Teen Pregnancy, pp. 5-6.
4. Albert, B., Brown, S.,& Flannigan, C. (Eds.) (2003), pg. 11.
5. Albert, B., Brown, S.,& Flannigan, C. (Eds.) (2003), pg. 11.
6. Albert, B., Brown, S.,& Flannigan, C. (Eds.) (2003), pg. 1.

Facts about Teenage Dating/Abuse/Violence:

Here are some things you should know:

- Early relationships are often unhealthy relationships.
- Teens that start dating early are much more likely to engage in sexual activity.
- Acquaintance rape is frequently unreported.
- Violence during teenage dating relationships is a predictor of potential violence in adult relationships.

Here are some additional facts:

- In a national survey, eight percent of students reported being forced to have sexual intercourse.[1] (Think about this – that is about 1 in 10!)
- About 72 percent of eighth and ninth grade students report that they are "dating."[6]
- Sexually abused girls are six times more likely to become pregnant and twice as likely to get an S.T.I.[6]
- In a nationwide survey, 9.4 percent of the students questioned reported being hit, slapped or physically hurt on purpose by their dating partner in the previous twelve months.[1]
- About one in five high school girls reports having been physically or sexually abused by a dating partner.[2]
- Eighty percent of teenagers believe verbal abuse is a serious issue for their age group.[2]
- Nearly four in five girls who have been victims of physical abuse in their dating relationships continue to date the abuser.[2]
- Nearly one in five teenage girls who have been in a relationship said that their boyfriend had threatened violence or self-harm in the event of a break-up.[2]
- Most teenage abuse occurs in the home of either the abuser or the victim.[2]
- Fifty-eight percent of rape victims reported being raped between the ages of 12 and 24.[3]
- Half of the reported date rapes occur among teenagers.[4]
- Seventy-seven percent of female and sixty-seven percent of male high school students endorse some form of sexual coercion, including unwanted kissing, hugging, genital contact, or sexual intercourse.

1. Youth dating Abuse and Statistics Risk Behavior Surveillance. *Morbidity and Mortality Weekly Report*. June 8th, 2012. Vol. 61. No. 4.
2. Lowen, Linda. Women's Issues Newsletter. 10 Facts about Teen Dating Violence-Teen Dating Abuse Statistics and about Choose Respect: Dating Abuse Fact Sheet, 2009.
3. Health Resources and Services Administration (HRSA) Maternal and Child Health Bureau, U.S. Department of Health and Human Services (HHS), 2002.
4. California Coalition Against Sexual Assault (CALCASA) 2002 Report: Research on Rape and Violence, http://www.uasasonoma.org/teensite/statistics.htm#Child/Teenpercent20Victimization, (Last Visited 10-1-04).
5. M. Jackson, F. Cram & F.W. Seymour, Journal of Family Violence, 2000.
6. Website: www.loveisrepect.org. Dating Abuse Statistics: Citations from Break the Cycle and or National Dating Abuse Helpline.

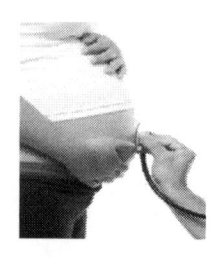

Facts about Adolescent Pregnancy:

Here are some things you should know:

- The United States has the highest rates for teenage pregnancy, teen births and teen abortion in the industrialized world.
- Most teenage mothers and fathers say they wish they would have waited to have their child until they were older or more prepared.
- Approximately fifty-seven percent of teenage pregnancies end in birth. Fourteen percent end in miscarriages. Nearly twenty-nine percent end in abortions.

Here are some additional facts:

- Teenagers that become pregnant are less likely to attend college. (Although teenage mothers are more likely to finish high school or earn their GED's than in the past.) [1]
- Nearly one million teenage girls get pregnant each year. Nearly four out of ten young women are pregnant at least once before they turn 20. [2]
- In a recent poll, 63 percent of teenagers (55 percent of boys, 72 percent of girls) who had sexual intercourse said they wish they had waited longer to have sex. [3]
- Children of teenage mothers are more likely to be born prematurely and at a low birth weight, which increases the chances of blindness, deafness, cognitive disabilities, cerebral palsy, and other disabilities. [4]

---

1. September 2006 report by the Guttmacher Institute
2. National Campaign to Prevent Teen Pregnancy. (1997) Whatever Happened to Childhood? The Problem of Teen Pregnancy in the United States. Washington, DC.
3. National Campaign to Prevent Teen Pregnancy. (2000) Not Just Another Thing to Do: Teens Talk About Sex, Regret and the Influence of their Parents. Washington, DC.
4. National Campaign to Prevent Teen Pregnancy. (1997) Whatever Happened to Childhood? The Problem of Teen Pregnancy in the United States. Washington, DC.

Facts about Adolescent Parenting:

Here are some things you should know:

- Ninety-three percent of pregnant adolescents have inadequate knowledge about parenting.
- 1.3 million children now live with a teenage mother. More than half are living with unmarried mothers. (There are 1.1 million teenage mothers in the U.S.)
- Almost half of the girls who give birth between the ages of 14 and 17 will be separated from the child's father within 5 years.
- Approximately 300,000 babies are born each year to teenage mothers who have not completed high school.

Here are some additional facts:

- Teenage mothers are more likely to live in poverty than women who delay childbearing. (More than 75 percent of all unmarried teens live on welfare within five years of the birth of their first child.) [1]
- About 64 percent of children born to an unmarried teenage high-school dropout live in poverty, compared to 7 percent of children born to women over the age of 20 who are married and are high school graduates. [2]
- A child born to a teenage mother is 50 percent more likely to repeat a grade in school, is more likely to perform poorly on standardized tests, and is more likely to drop out before finishing high school. [3]
- Sons of teenage fathers are 13 percent more likely than their peers with older parents to end up in prison. [4]
- Children born to mothers age fifteen and younger are twice as likely to become a victim of child abuse or neglect within the first five years of life than children born to mothers age twenty to twenty-one. [5]

---

1. Teenage Pregnancy Fact Sheet, March of Dimes Foundation, March 2009.
2. "Dropouts Graduate to Jail": 1 in 10 in U.S., the Commercial Appeal, October 12, 2009.
3. "Dropouts to Cost Tennessee Billions," The Commercial Appeal, October 4, 2009.
4. "Editorial: Region Leads in Teen Births" The Commercial Appeal, January 9, 2009.
5. George, R.M., & Lee, B.J. (1997), "Abuse and Neglect of the Children," in R. Maynard (Ed.), Kids having kids. Washington, DC: The Urban Institute Press.

Facts about S.T.I.s / S.T.D.s

They are called S.T.I.s, sexual transmitted infections or S.T.D.s, sexually transmitted diseases. Historically they were referred to as V.D.s (venereal diseases), and are really just different names for the same diseases and infections. We'll refer to them as S.T.I.s.

Here are some things you should know:

- Millions of teens are infected with S.T.I.s each year.
- Once every 15 seconds, someone in the U.S. is contracting a S.T.I.
- One in 17 teens will get an S.T.I. every year.
- There are at least three S.T.I.s **for which there is no cure.**
- Approximately two out of 1,000 college students are infected with HIV and don't know it.

Here are some additional facts:

- Nearly half of the 19 million new S.T.I.s contracted each year affect people ages 15 to 24. [1]
- Human papillomavirus (HPV) is the most common S.T.I. among teens, with infection rates reaching 35 percent of 14- to 19-year-olds. *Currently there are two vaccines (Gardasil and Cervarix) that protect against strains of HPV associated with cervical cancer and genital warts.* [2]
- Thirty-seven percent of young men and 70 percent of young women had an S.T.I. test in the past year. [3]
- Over 34,000 young people ages 13 to 24 were estimated to be living with HIV in the U.S. in 2009. [4]

---

1. Weinstock, H., Berman, S., Cates, W., Sexually transmitted diseases among American youth: incidence and prevalence estimates, 2000. *Perspectives on Sexual and Reproductive Health 2004; 36(1): 6-10.*
2. *CDC, Sexually Transmitted Disease Surveillance, 2012.*
3. Cunningham, S. "Relationships Between perceived STD-Related Stigma, STD-Related Shame, STD Screening among Household Sample of Adolescents." PSRH, 2009.
4. CDC, HIV/AIDS Surveillance in Adolescents and Young Adults, 2012.

Facts about Sexual Abuse and Technology

Here are some things you should know:

- In the United States, 1.8 million adolescents have been victims of sexual assault.
- Most sexual abusers are acquaintances of the victim. As many as 47 percent are members of the victim's family or extended family.
- "Sexting" (exchange of explicit sexual messages or images by mobile phones) can be a form of sexual abuse.

Here are some additional facts:

- As many as one in three girls and one in seven boys will be sexually abused at some point in their childhood. [1]
- Thirty-three percent of sexual assaults occur when the victim is between the ages of 12 and 17. [2]
- Teenagers 16 to 19 years of age were three and a half times more likely than the general population to be victims of rape, attempted rape, or sexual assault. [3]
- One in 25 youths received an online sexual solicitation in which the solicitor tried to make an offline contact. [4]
- In more than one-fourth of online sexual solicitation incidents, solicitors asked youths for sexual photographs of themselves. [4]
- Fifteen percent of cell-owning teenagers (12 to 17 years old) say they have received sexually suggestive (nude or seminude) images of someone they know via text. [5]
- Twenty-two percent of teenage girls and 18 percent of teenage boys have sent or posted nude or seminude pictures or videos of themselves. [6]
- Thirty-six percent of teenage girls and 39 percent of teenage boys say it is common for nude or seminude photos to get shared with someone other than the intended recipient. [6]

---

1. Briere, J. and Eliot, D.M., "Prevalence and Psychological Sequence of Self-Reported Childhood Physical and Sexual Abuse in General Population." Child Abuse and Neglect, 2003, Vol. 27, Issue 10, pp.1205-1222.
2. "Sexual Assault of Young Children as Reported to Law Enforcement: Victim, Incident, and Offender Characteristics." U.S. Department of Justice, Bureau of Justice Stats. 2000.
3. "National Crime Victimization Survey." U.S. Department of Justice, Bureau of Justice Stats. 1996.

4. Wolak, Janis, J.D., Finkelhor, David, Mitchell, Kimberly J. and Ybarra, Michele, "Online Predators and Their Victims; Myths, Realities and Implications for Prevention and Treatment." American Psychologist, 2008, 63:111-128.
5. Lenhart, Amanda, "Teens and Sexting" Pew Internet and American Life Project, December 15th, 2009.
6. The National Campaign to Prevent Unplanned Pregnancy, "Sex and Tech-Results from a Survey of Teens and Young Adults," (Nov. 1-2012).

"Forced Topics" For Discussion with Pre-teens

There are several "Forced Topics" I recommend that all parents discuss with their pre-teen at some time during their adolescent development. The recommended topics and issues are listed below, followed by definitions of specific topics about which I want to avoid misunderstanding of the meaning assigned to them. I encourage parents to find the appropriate times to "force" a discussion of these topics during their child's pre-teen and teenage years.

Here are some basic communication tips to keep in mind while discussing these and other issues with your child:

- **Seize the moment:** When a TV program, movie, or music video raises issues about life's decisions, use them as discussion-starters.
- **Keep it on the "low-key:"** Don't pressure your child – keep the door open. If he or she isn't open for discussion at the time you want talk, say, "Sometime I'd like to discuss that issue with you."
- **Be honest:** If something comes up in a conversation that surprises, shocks, or dismays you, deal with it calmly so that your child will continue to share sensitive information with you.
- **Be direct:** Clearly state your opinions and feelings about the issues of concern. Present the risks of objectionable behaviors calmly and objectively.
- **Consider your child's point of view:** Don't lecture your child or use scare tactics. Be empathetic, understanding their pressures, challenges and concerns.
- **Move beyond the facts:** Provide accurate and reliable facts but avoid sounding like a doctoral research candidate. Raise moral and ethical questions consistent within your values. Talk about what constitutes responsible behavior.
- **Invite more discussion:** When finished with any topic, say "I'm glad you came to me," or "I'm glad we had this discussion," or "I'm really happy we can talk like this; let's do it again soon."

You can strengthen your bonds with your teens with good communication. In chapter 11, I offer an interactive activity called "Definitions Missing." You can try one of two interactive options. In the first you will create a "discussion jar" in which you will place pieces of paper, each containing one of the "forced topics." At a mutually agreed time every month or so, a topic can be drawn from the jar and discussed. In the second option you will take a more directed approach to your discussions. You can keep the doors of communication open by discussing these and any other topics with your child on a regular basis. Remember to **Enjoy**!

"Forced Topics" for Discussion with PRE-TEENS

Commitment	Love
Contraception	Cyber-bullying
Infatuation	Dignity
Will power	Empathy
Restraint	Seriousness of relationships
Abstinence	Consequences of early sexual activity
Respect for self	Goals and unwanted teenage pregnancies
Respect for someone of "interest"	Virginity
Sexual differences/Identity	Life skills
Accountability	Values needed in healthy relationships
Consequences	Responsibilities in healthy relationships
"Sex" vs. "Sexual activity" vs. "Sexual intercourse"	Sexual activity continuum
Alcohol use	Drug use
Smoking/Chewing tobacco	Bullying
Eating Disorders	Self-Injury or Cutting
Depression/suicide	Coping
Death or Loss	Qualities in a healthy relationship
"Safe" vs. "Safer" sex	Texting/Sexting/Power of social media
Boundaries	

Definitions of "Forced Topics"

Although some of these topics need no definition, I will define those that may require some clarification and understanding.

Commitment: A pledge, a promise, a covenant, an agreement or a vow that binds.

Love: A genuine feeling of warmth, affection, attachment, devotion and/or attraction to another person.

Contraception: Deliberate prevention of conception or impregnation.

Cyber-bullying: Bullying that occurs using any form of social media.

Infatuation: When someone is fascinated, enchanted, enraptured, enamored with another person often because of a few traits or characteristics.

Dignity: Having the quality of being worthy of esteem or respect.

Will power: The internal mental and emotional power to practice restraint.

Empathy: The ability to put oneself in another person's "shoes" and feel what they are feeling or experiencing.

Restraint: The power to hold back and not take part in a given activity.

Seriousness of relationships

Abstinence

Consequences of early sexual activity

Respect for self: To consider oneself worthy of respect. A healthy regard for one's own worth.

Goals and unwanted teenage pregnancies

Respect for someone of "interest": To acknowledge the worth of another person. A sincere appreciation of another person.

Virginity: The quality or state of being celibate. Not having engaged in sexual intercourse.

Sexual differences: The variety of gender differences and sexual manifestations within the human species.

Life skills: Specific actions/behaviors that promote effective navigation of life's challenges and opportunities.

Accountability

Values need in healthy relationships

Consequences

Responsibilities in healthy relationships

"Sex" vs. "sexual activity" vs. "sexual intercourse:"

> **"Sex"** refers to your gender – male or female.
>
> **"Sexual activity"** is another ambiguous term that needs to be clarified. It describes any behavior that stimulates another person – physically or emotionally.
>
> **"Sexual intercourse"** refers to coitus, or the physical act by which humans reproduce.

Sexual activity continuum: A pattern of sexual behaviors progressing through stages from mere infatuation to passionate petting and finally sexual intercourse.

Alcohol use

Drug use

Smoking/ chewing tobacco

Bullying

Eating Disorders

Self-injury / Cutting

Depression /Stress/ Coping

Death / Loss

Qualities in a healthy relationship

"Safe" vs. "safer" sex:

"Safe sex" refers to sexual intercourse while using any of a variety of prophylactic (non-chemical) contraceptive devices. The most common are male and female condoms. *I contend that there is no "safe sex" for teens except abstinence since there is always a possibility that the prophylactic device will fail and a pregnancy will occur.*

"Safer sex" refers to having sexual intercourse while using various chemical methods of contraception (birth control pills, implants, etc.) to prevent a pregnancy.

Texting/Sexting/Power of social media

A Final Word

In concluding this chapter on communication it is important to address one of the barriers to healthy communication, social media – Facebook, Instagram, computers, texting, cell phones, TV, video games, etc. According to a 2010 Kaiser Family Foundation study of 8- to 18-year-olds, "today's teens spend more than 7.5 hours per day consuming media.

Text messaging has become the mainstay of communication in most homes. It also has become an addiction. Two months before I retired as a public school health educator, I was teaching a unit on addictions. During the class period I witnessed one of my students tearing up as I taught. Not wanting to embarrass her, I waited to address her until the completion of the class. At the end of the hour she remained after the others left. I approached her out of concern and asked what was wrong. She said, "based on your definition of addiction today in class, I am addicted to texting." I asked why she believed that. She said she had been receiving approximately 200 texts a day and felt she HAD to respond to each and every one of them! How sad that a thirteen-year-old young lady was addicted to her phone and her text messages.

As parents, if you are communicating some of the time with your teens or pre-teens online, you should know the online chat abbreviations. To become aware of some of those, I would recommend this site: www.webopedia.com/quick_ref/textmessageabbreviation.asp.

With that said however, I can't emphasize too strongly the need to limit the amount of texting you do with your pre-teens. They need to talk to you face to face. If they are to know how to create strong relationships they will need your example. Talk to them directly and show them, by example, how to talk to friends, relatives, and others directly.

Parents…..Lead on…..!

Chapter 2

General parenting suggestions to "set the stage"

There is no such thing as a perfect parent. We are all practicing parents, doing what we know; providing, caring for, and loving our children while we attempt to raise happy, healthy, successful, and responsible adults.

There are many factors that may influence the way we function as a parent. Likewise our children's peers, teachers, relatives, siblings, life experiences, the media, our society all play a significant role in their development. However, the role we play as parents is crucial to how they will deal with *all* of those other influences. Parenting is a full time job. We need to ask ourselves if we are investing as much dedication and commitment in our children as we are in our regular career.

I have developed many strategies while working with pre-teenagers and their parents in my 30 years of public school teaching and my work in drug and alcohol rehabilitation. While raising our own two children I have been able to practice these strategies and add to them as well. Parents and teens have stated that these strategies have had a positive effect on their relationships and contributed to their eventual success. I am going to share them with you knowing that you may already be doing some of the things I'll suggest. Others will be new to you and you will want to incorporate them into your existing parenting style.

1. **First realize you are not perfect**. Guilt can burden you and cause you to retreat as a parent. The things you know about parenting you learned from your parents, from observing other parents and from your own experiences. Some might be good; some might not be so good. This book is premised on the belief that you are doing the best you know for your children but you could always do better.

    Every parent makes mistakes, but they don't have to be fatal! Dealing with adolescence is tough for the child *and* for the parent. The things you will learn in this book will help prepare you for those difficult times so you can deal with them with an understanding attitude.

2. **Learn to take care yourself.** In order to have the needed energy and proper attitude to be a good parent – and spouse for that matter – you need to take care of yourself first. Generally, we take care of ourselves last. It should be the other way around.

3. **Tell your children often that you love them.** End every "text" and phone call with "Love you!" Hold them long enough while looking them in the eyes to say, "I love you…"

    When they do things wrong, show them you still *love them* even though you do not like what *they did.* Unconditional love is paramount when it comes to raising teens. Saying you love your pre-teen is one thing; regularly showing them with your behaviors and your actions is much different! *Say and show* is to the parenting game what *show and tell* was in elementary school!

4. **Remind your child of his or her positive traits.** Also, for children ages 4-10 create a nightly ritual. Before you put them to bed each night, have them tell you one thing they like about themselves and one thing they are looking forward to the next day. This builds self-confidence and allows them to go to bed with hope every night! Self-confidence and hope are very important assets your teens need while developing into adulthood. Self-confidence is important when they are dealing with internal pressures (pressures put on themselves within their own mind) and external pressures (pressures put on by their peers, our society, media, etc.). When appropriate, discuss how your child might handle different situations when their self-confidence is high and those same situations when they sense that it is low. Regularly catch your children being good and show them your appreciation.

5. **Spend time truly listening – non-judgmentally – to your children.** If they feel uncomfortable talking with you at first, suggest that they write their thoughts, ideas and concerns on paper and then share them with you. Teach them to listen. Great family discussions occur when you have two basic rules: first, only one person speaks at a time, and secondly, no voices raise – period! Teach them to paraphrase what each other has said. Paraphrasing is putting what was just stated into your own words and repeating it to make sure that what you heard is what the other person meant to say. Start with, "so what you said was…."

6. **Practice the necessary steps to effective communication.** Keep your voice calm. Look at the other person's eyes intermittently. Sit at the same level with them. Sit fairly close to them, and, if possible, touch them as you talk. Practice

talking AND listening! Don't get into "shouting matches" – they become more about power than about understanding each other. To find time for communication you may have to limit the time your child spends playing video games, "working" on the computer, texting and watching television. Consider allowing them to "buy" back some time after they have had a really good, stimulating discussion with you! Don't forget to occasionally ask your teen to help you think about a particular problem you may be facing!

7. **Always show interest in your child's activities.** Be supportive of their many "what I want to be" career choices. Encourage them to learn new things and try new experiences.

8. **Get to know your child's friends.** The integrity of your child's friends plays a big role in the decisions your child will make as she or he moves through the teenage years. Make your home a welcome place for your child's friends. Get to know their family situation. Form an alliance network with their parents. If your child is staying at the home of a friend, follow up with a phone call to the parents or show up to make sure they are where they said they would be. Encourage social groups that include both boys and girls! Notice I didn't say cliques, but social groups that invite others in and let others leave when they decide to leave.

9. **Be alert to, and make use of "teachable moments."** Regularly, use age-appropriate newspaper articles, TV news stories, movies, magazine articles, global issues, etc. to initiate discussions of "life-issues."

10. **Help your child set goals.** Whether they are short-term goals for the week, month, year, or long-term goals for their life, they need your help. Write a "bucket list" of wishes you have for them and share it with them. Encourage them to write their own. I would suggest writing a family bucket list as well! These are valuable things to do as a family before the teens leave home to start their own lives. Research clearly shows that people who write their goals down, making them visible, attain more of them in their lives.

11. **Support your child's growing independence.** Trust her or him as much as possible, but allow for minor mistakes. Learn when to loosen those apron strings and when to pull them back. Give them specific duties and insist that they be responsible for performing them correctly and on time.

12. **Provide consequences for failures and mis-behavior.** Consequences need to be a part of your child's life just as they are a part of yours. It is critical that you do what you say you are going to do for a consequence. Whether it is a consequence you decide arbitrarily or one mutually agreed upon doesn't matter. But, be careful if you set a consequence when you are angry or in a power struggle with your child. Once your child knows that your consequences are negotiable, or that you may relent on them, he or she will play "Let's make a Deal" FOREVER! Realize it is okay to say "no." Sometimes you will even feel worse than your teen by insisting on the consequence, but you have to stick to it, explain your reasoning, and let time heal the pain for both of you. Consequences are a fact of life, and pre-teens need to understand that as soon as they can. Parents need to know the difference between punishment and discipline – use discipline, avoid punishment!

13. **Be quick to ask for forgiveness.** Letting your children know you can be wrong and you want to "make it right" can be an extremely valuable life lesson. Demonstrate for them ways to make up after a quarrel or disagreement. And remember, agreeing to disagree is a viable conflict resolution tool!

14. **Have a sense of humor with your pre-teen.** Create opportunities to laugh together. Humor (laughter) is the spice of life. Teens that appreciate good humor develop healthier relationships later in life. I would bet that humor was in the top five characteristics you valued in your future mate!

15. **Communicate with the parents of your pre-teens, and with their teachers.** Let your child know what you are hearing. When you hear positive things, immediately share those compliments with your pre-teen. When your pre-teen knows you are in touch with other adults in their life it will influence decisions he or she makes in the future.

16. **Don't get into shouting matches with your pre-teen.** At times, it is extremely difficult to avoid doing so. Try to maintain eye contact and speak in a low, calming and caring tone of voice. If an argument escalates, suggest a cooling off period and choose a time to continue the discussion later. Know that the silent treatment doesn't work! Don't adopt the immature idea, "I'm not going to say anything to them any longer…" Regularly scheduled family meetings are an effective way for everyone to share what they are thinking about or experiencing. Family meetings help prevent big arguments and blow-ups. And remember my two ground rules: One person speaks at a time and no voice-raising.

17. **Show Respect for your pre-teen by what you say and how you act, regardless of the situation.** Children need to feel valued despite any disagreement or disappointment. Your children learn to respect themselves and others by *being respected.*

18. **Hug your child often.** Even though they may feel some discomfort in front of their peers, hug them anyway. Researchers say that we need approximately twelve physical touches a day, and some of the research specifically states that pre-teens who don't get sufficient physical parental contact compensate by growing up to be more physically violent and/or sexually active as a teen.

19. **Spend quality time with your children.** Do things with several of your children together. And do things one-on-one with each of your children. (Taking them to sporting events or practices, or music lessons or concerts doesn't count.) I suggest having a family night, one night a week, in which your family does something together – NO MATTER WHAT! Make it a tradition. By the way, families that regularly eat together have a stronger family bond. Although it is hard to accomplish, eating one meal as day together can pay big dividends in your relationship with your child.

20. **Teach your pre-teens how to problem-solve and make decisions.** Problem-solve with them on a regular basis, asking for their input, whenever possible. I will expand on these two life skills in chapter 8.

21. **Discuss your feelings often.** When you share your feelings with your child it opens the door for him or her to share feelings with you. Regularly tell them how you feel. Discussions like this provide excellent opportunities for you to reveal your values to your child.

22. **Practice what you preach.** Your children really are like little ducklings. They will do what you do as they grow toward independence. That's sometimes a scary thought. Sincerely and genuinely model the behaviors every parent should want to see in their child: clean, respectful language, empathy, sympathy, compassion, respect, open-mindedness, etc.

23. **Set reasonable limits with your pre-teens that allow them to earn your trust**. Emphasize that trust is an ongoing process accomplished over a long period of time, but it can be lost very quickly and easily. Once trust has been lost it will take time to rebuild it.

24. **NEVER end the day angry with your pre-teen.** Let them know that though you may disagree with them, or you may have been angry with them, you nonetheless still love them.

25. **Practice empathy.** Put yourself in your pre-teens shoes. Ask, "How might he or she be feeling?" Try to remember "back in the day" and how you felt. It will open your eyes to a better understanding of your pre-teen and make your communication with him or her more effective.

"PARENT ON"… AND LEAD AS A MORE KNOWLEDGEABLE, CARING PARENT!

You say
when...where...how ...why?

Chapter 3

Practical suggestions for *when*, *where*, *how* and *why* to use this interactive work book with your pre-teen.

WHEN

Actually, the sooner you can begin the discussions, the better. The best ages for sound, relevant and interactive discussions are between ages 11 to 14. All of your discussions and interactive activities should definitely occur sometime between the ages of 11 to 18. I believe you will achieve more success communicating with your pre-teen by working one on one, using the topic discussion activities and the interactive activities. Of course, this depends on the level of trust, comfort and communication you have with your child. Eliminate distractions during your discussion and work times (no video, no phone for texting, no TV, no working on homework, etc.). Set deadlines, specific dates by which certain topic discussions and certain activities must be completed, i.e. by the middle school dance, homecoming, prom, etc. Make discussion times relaxed, private and non-threatening. Having a treat such as popcorn, maybe hot chocolate or ice cream, etc. will work! Teens are more relaxed if they can talk while they eat!

WHERE

Find appropriate and comfortable places to initiate discussion. Talk about the topics or work on the activities at pre-determined places. These may occur when just you and your pre-teen are in your car when you are driving for some distance. Other appropriate places include a restaurant, after a movie, sitting around a campfire together, at home after viewing a TV show that dealt with a pertinent teen issue or in your pre-teen's room after attending a church service together. A fishing boat could provide an opportunity for discussion. It could be in a mutually agreed upon room or part of the house where it is quiet and private. Discussions can also occur on a planned getaway for the day or even a weekend. Anywhere that the two of you feel comfortable and relaxed and have adequate time is a good place for a discussion.

HOW TO USE

I recommend that you read the first 10 chapters of this book and then decide on a plan to work with your pre-teen. If possible, plan single parent discussions first and then slowly include your spouse or significant other later. Decide whether to begin by discussing topics on a weekly, bi-monthly or monthly basis. Choose any of the activities from chapter 10 in any order and keep them in a folder entitled, "(Your pre-teens name) Life Plans." It helps to develop a timeline of agreed upon dates by which particular discussion topics and activities must be completed before your teen can get her or his driver's license, begin dating, go to prom, etc.! By making the timeline a mutual decision, the goals will be put in a positive light allowing the teen to work toward desired outcomes.

WHY

Sharing this information with your pre-teen is critical to their development and to the success of their life-long relationships. It is imperative for you as the parent to read the first ten chapters. There you will discover the information you'll need to impart to your pre-teen. Why pre-teens? I believe they are more impressionable and ready for this information than they will be in their teen years. Why 11 to 14? For the most part 11- to 14-year-olds haven't yet faced the pressures and temptations they will face in the years just ahead of them. You will be more successful working from a preventative position rather than a reactive one. I have seen the ideas outlined in these chapters work with the many teens I have taught in my classroom and counseled in treatment centers.

Priceless Gifts for Your Teen!

Chapter 4

What makes teens successful?

Eighteen years as a parent and thirty years in health education has convinced me that there is a basic formula for raising successful teens. I'll share it with you as a mathematical formula. I believe that pre-teens opportunities for success are dramatically increased if they and their parents understand and use the following formula:

**KNOWLEDGE + LIFE SKILLS + ASSET DEVELOPMENT =
AN EMPOWERED, HAPPY, HEALTHY AND SUCCESSFUL TEEN**

Our teens need to have specific knowledge about life's major decisions in order to succeed. That is why I have suggested you start by discussing the topics found in chapter 1. That is also why I am a firm supporter of K-12 health education in our school systems. It builds a foundation for everything else they learn in their 12 years of education. For example, what if your teen is at the top in their class, but is heavily involved with drugs, sad and lonely with no healthy relationships in their life? What if their personal goal was to go to college after high school but an unintended pregnancy renders them unable to afford college, or the responsibilities of parenting leaves them without the time or energy to commit to an education?

I have enumerated life skills in chapter nine that teens need to know and utilize in order to be successful in life. In addition to those specific life skills, pre-teens/teens need to be encouraged and assisted in acquiring specific developmental assets that will help them succeed in life. These assets are heavily researched, specific characteristics, traits and/or "building blocks" needed to insure a happy, healthy and successful life. I will address some very relevant and useful research from the Search Institute in Minneapolis, Minnesota and lay out the 40 assets they have identified later in this chapter.

Once a teen has learned about major decisions they will face in life, and has acquired the necessary life skills to assist them in making those decisions, they can then effectively begin to acquire these 40 proven assets. This "mathematical life formula" equates to insuring a *POWER-FULL* teenager, prepared to experience a life full of health, happiness and success.

Before I share the 40 assets that lead to a successful life, let me explain their origin.

The Search Institute, in Minneapolis Minnesota, is a research foundation that has studied youth behavior for over fifty years. In 1990, Search Institute released a framework of 40 Developmental Assets which identifies a set of skills, experiences, relationships, and behaviors that enable young people to develop into successful and contributing adults. Over the following two decades, the Developmental Assets framework and approach to youth development became the most frequently cited and widely utilized in the world, creating what Stanford University's William Damon described as a "sea change" in adolescent development.

Data collected from Search Institute surveys of more than 4 million children and youth from all backgrounds and situations has consistently demonstrated that the more Developmental Assets young people acquire, the better are their chances of succeeding in school and becoming happy, healthy, and contributing members of their communities and society. They have identified, in their research, 40 traits, characteristics and/or building blocks that youth need in order to increase their opportunities for a healthy, happy and successful life. Teens with a higher number of assets (closer to 40) make better decisions, are much happier and are more successful in life. The opposite is true as well. The interesting piece of their research is that these 40 assets are all focused on **positive behaviors** instead of negative ones. Twenty of the assets, called internal assets, must be developed by the teen on their own. The other 20, called external assets, need to be learned, directly or indirectly, from external sources, including parents, family members, the community, churches and definitely, their school.

The research clearly shows that unhealthy behaviors diminish as the teen acquires more of the forty assets. Conversely, teens with fewer assets have a greater likelihood of developing unhealthy and destructive behaviors. According to the Search Institute, studies of more than four million young people consistently show that the more assets young people have, the less likely they are to engage in a wide range of high-risk behaviors and the more likely they are to thrive. Research shows that youth with the least assets are most likely to engage in four different patterns of high-risk behavior: problem alcohol use, violence, illicit drug use, and unhealthy sexual activity. Those with higher levels of assets, tend to do well in school, to be engaged in their community, and to value diversity.

The positive power of these forty assets is evident across all cultural and socioeconomic groups of youth in the United States as well as other parts of the world. Interestingly, the degree to which a teen has acquired or not acquired these assets proves to be a better predictor of success or failure than economic status, family stability, or other demographic differences. Sadly, the average American teen has acquired only 18 assets.

The next two pages show, graphically, the specific information discussed in this chapter. The first set of graphs shows the average number of assets acquired by grade and gender and the percentage of youth that have acquired a specific number of assets. The next page clearly reveals the power of assets. You will notice that the higher numbers protect your pre-teen from high risk behaviors and, at the same time, promote positive attitudes and healthy behaviors.

The Challenge Facing Communities

While the assets are powerful shapers of young people's lives and choices, too few young people experience many of these assets. Twenty-five of the 40 assets are experienced by less than half of the young people surveyed.

Average Number of Assets by Grade and Gender

The average young person surveyed experiences only 18 of the 40 assets. In general, older youth have lower average levels of assets than younger youth. And boys experience fewer assets than girls.

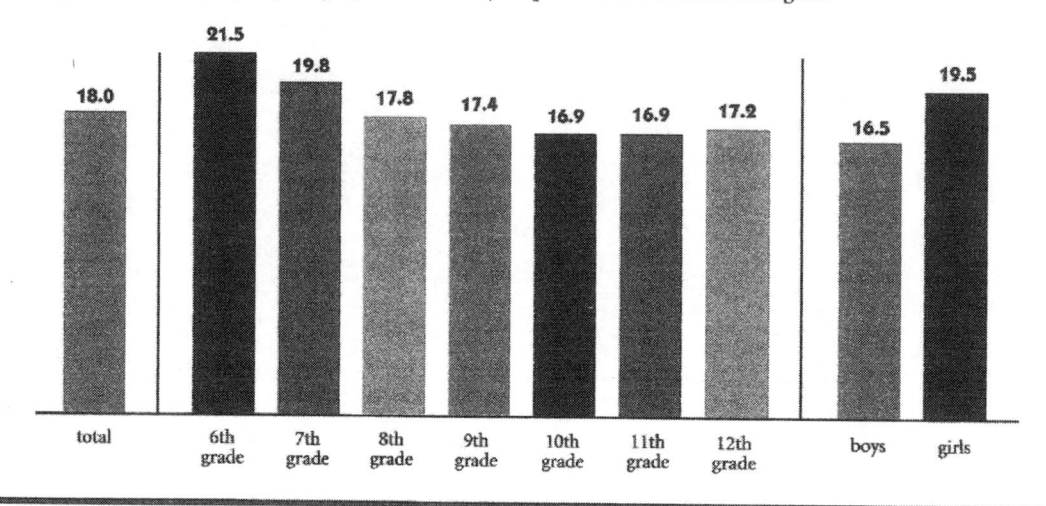

Category	Average
total	18.0
6th grade	21.5
7th grade	19.8
8th grade	17.8
9th grade	17.4
10th grade	16.9
11th grade	16.9
12th grade	17.2
boys	16.5
girls	19.5

Youth with Different Levels of Assets

Ideally, all youth would experience at least 31 of these 40 assets. Yet, as this chart shows, only 8 percent of youth experience this level of assets. Sixty-two percent experience fewer than 20 of the assets.

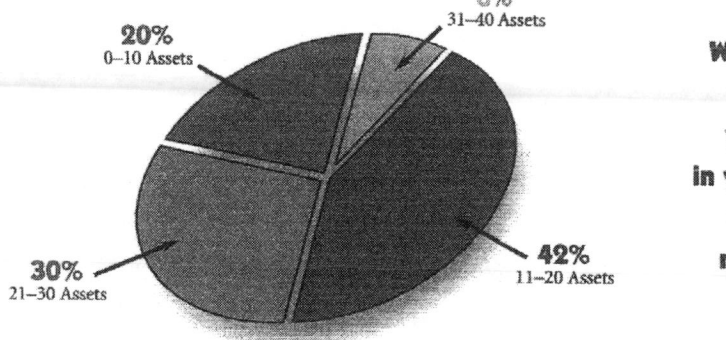

- 8% — 31–40 Assets
- 20% — 0–10 Assets
- 30% — 21–30 Assets
- 42% — 11–20 Assets

What goal would you set for young people in your community, organization, neighborhood, or family?

The Power of Assets

On one level, the 40 developmental assets represent everyday wisdom about positive experiences and characteristics for young people. In addition, Search Institute research has found that these assets are powerful influences on adolescent behavior—both protecting young people from many different problem behaviors and promoting positive attitudes and behaviors. This power is evident across all cultural and socioeconomic groups of youth. There is also evidence from other research that assets may have the same kind of power for younger children.

Protecting Youth from High-Risk Behaviors

Assets have tremendous power to protect youth from many different harmful or unhealthy choices. To illustrate, these charts show that youth with the most assets are least likely to engage in four different patterns of high-risk behavior. *(For definitions of each problem behavior, see Page 7.)*

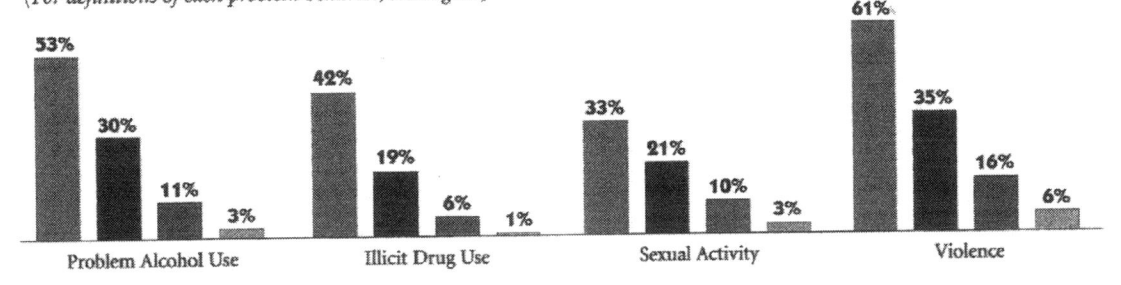

Behavior	0-10 Assets	11-20 Assets	21-30 Assets	31-40 Assets
Problem Alcohol Use	53%	30%	11%	3%
Illicit Drug Use	42%	19%	6%	1%
Sexual Activity	33%	21%	10%	3%
Violence	61%	35%	16%	6%

The same kind of impact is evident with many other problem behaviors, including tobacco use, depression and attempted suicide, antisocial behavior, school problems, driving and alcohol, and gambling.

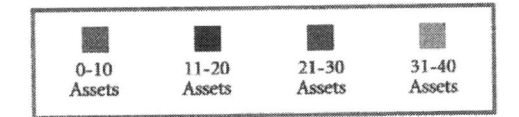

Promoting Positive Attitudes and Behaviors

In addition to protecting youth from negative behaviors, having more assets increases the chances that young people will have positive attitudes and behaviors, as these charts show. *(For definitions of each thriving behavior, see Page 7.)*

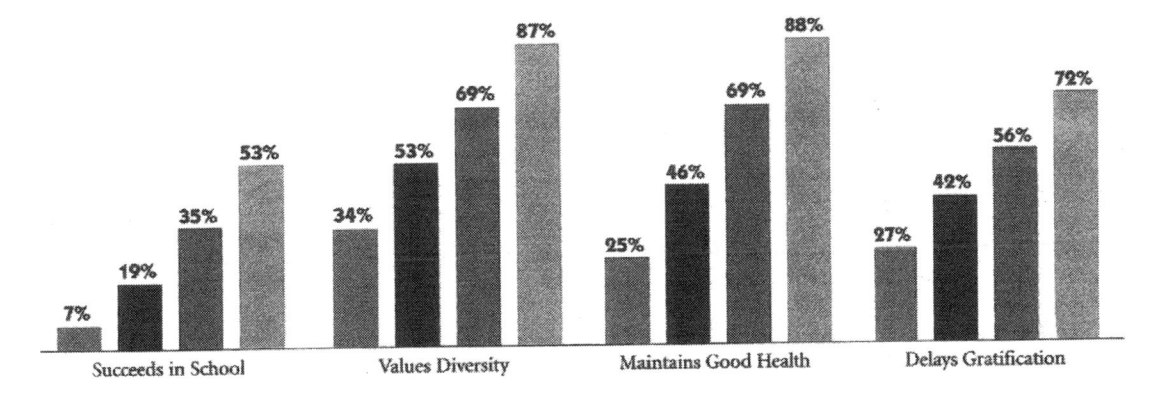

Behavior	0-10 Assets	11-20 Assets	21-30 Assets	31-40 Assets
Succeeds in School	7%	19%	35%	53%
Values Diversity	34%	53%	69%	87%
Maintains Good Health	25%	46%	69%	88%
Delays Gratification	27%	42%	56%	72%

You may go to the Search Institute's website at www.search-institute.org to become better informed about the 40 assets and to peruse other materials. But now, here are the 40 assets that insure a happy, healthy and successful teenager.

40 Developmental Assets®
for Middle Childhood (ages 8-12)

Search Institute® has identified the following building blocks of healthy development – **Developmental Assets®** – that help young people grow up healthy, caring, and responsible.

1. **Family support**—Family life provides high levels of love and support.
2. **Positive family communication**—Parent(s) and child communicate positively. Child feels comfortable seeking advice and counsel from parent(s).
3. **Other adult relationships**—Child receives support from adults other than her or his parent(s).
4. **Caring neighborhood**—Child experiences caring neighbors.
5. **Caring school climate**—Relationships with teachers and peers provide a caring, encouraging environment.
6. **Parent involvement in schooling**—Parent(s) are actively involved in helping the child succeed in school.
7. **Community values youth**—Child feels valued and appreciated by adults in the community.
8. **Children as resources**—Child is included in decisions at home and in the community.
9. **Service to others**—Child has opportunities to help others in the community.
10. **Safety**—Child feels safe at home, at school, and in his or her neighborhood.
11. **Family boundaries**—Family has clear and consistent rules and consequences and monitors the child's whereabouts.
12. **School Boundaries**—School provides clear rules and consequences.
13. **Neighborhood boundaries**—Neighbors take responsibility for monitoring the child's behavior.
14. **Adult role models**—Parent(s) and other adults in the child's family, as well as nonfamily adults, model positive, responsible behavior.
15. **Friends**—Child's closest friends model positive, responsible behavior.
16. **High expectations**—Parent(s) and teachers expect the child to do her or his best at school and in other activities.
17. **Creative activities**—Child participates in music, art, drama, or creative writing two or more times per week.
18. **Child programs**—Child participates two or more times per week in co-curricular school activities or structured community programs for children..
19. **Religious community**—Child attends religious programs or services one or more times per week.

20. **Time at home**—Child spends some time most days both in high-quality interaction with parents and doing things at home other than watching TV or playing video games.
21. **Achievement Motivation**—Child is motivated and strives to do well in school.
22. **Learning Engagement**—Child is responsive, attentive, and actively engaged in learning at school and enjoys participating in learning activities outside of school.
23. **Homework**—Child usually hands in homework on time.
24. **Bonding to school**—Child cares about teachers and other adults at school.
25. **Reading for Pleasure**—Child enjoys and engages in reading for fun most days of the week.
26. **Caring**—Parent(s) tell the child it is important to help other people.
27. **Equality and social justice**—Parent(s) tell the child it is important to speak up for equal rights for all people.
28. **Integrity**—Parent(s) tell the child it is important to stand up for one's beliefs.
29. **Honesty**—Parent(s) tell the child it is important to tell the truth.
30. **Responsibility**—Parent(s) tell the child it is important to accept personal responsibility for behavior.
31. **Healthy Lifestyle**—Parent(s) tell the child it is important to have good health habits and an understanding of healthy sexuality.
32. **Planning and decision making**—Child thinks about decisions and is usually happy with results of her or his decisions.
33. **Interpersonal Competence**—Child cares about and is affected by other people's feelings, enjoys making friends, and, when frustrated or angry, tries to calm her or himself.
34. **Cultural Competence**—Child knows and is comfortable with people of different racial, ethnic, and cultural backgrounds and with her or his own cultural identity.
35. **Resistance skills**—Child can stay away from people who are likely to get them in trouble. They are able to say no to things that are not healthy, legal and safe.
36. **Child seeks to resolve conflict nonviolently**—Child tries to resolve conflicts non-violently
37. **Personal power**—Child feels he or she has some influence over things that happen in her or his life.
38. **Self-esteem**—Child likes and is proud to be the person that he or she is.
39. **Sense of purpose**—Child sometimes thinks about what life means and whether there is a purpose for her or his life.
40. **Positive view of personal future**—Child is optimistic about her or his personal future.

Copyright © 2003, 2006 by Search Institute, 615 First Avenue N.E., Suite 125, Minneapolis, MN 55413; 800-888-7828; www.search-institute.org. All Rights Reserved. These are registered trademarks of Search Institute: Search Institute®, Developmental Assets® and Healthy Communities • Healthy Youth®.

So when it's "gift time" for your pre-teens' birthdays, Christmas or other holidays ask yourselves as parents if you are giving them the three most priceless gifts – the knowledge, life skills, and assets needed to live a healthy, happy and successful life. By now you can see that these 40 developmental assets are a critical component in the em*POWER*ment of your child, leading to that kind of life.

KNOWLEDGE + LIFE SKILLS + ASSET DEVELOPMENT =
AN EM*POWER*ED, HAPPY, HEALTHY AND SUCCESSFUL TEEN!

Setting Goals for Success......!

Chapter 5

Empowering your pre-teen with goals, dreams and wishes— writing "bucket lists"

One of the 40 developmental assets was the ability to plan ahead and make choices. Teens need goals, dreams and wishes to acquire hope. Hope provides optimism. Optimism develops their positive attitudes. The research is clear that youth who have goals (preferably written goals) choose fewer unhealthy behaviors. Did you know that 87% of our population does not have goals! Approximately 10% of the population has goals but only 3% of our population has written down their goals. And here's the interesting piece about that fact: the 3% who have written their goals accomplish 50-100 times more than the others who either don't have goals or don't write them down!

As a former health educator, I regularly gave my students an assignment regarding their goals. I asked them to brainstorm and list 15 things they'd like to do or be and list any places they'd like to visit before they die. A middle school student quickly completed her assignment to my great amazement. Little Sarah came the next day with her list on a long sheet of the old connected computer paper. Remember the paper with the holes on the edges? She came with a list of 260 goals! She was extremely excited about her list and said she and her mother planned to go to a department store after school and purchase 275 brightly colored 3 x 5 note cards. She explained that she was going to write each goal on a separate card and then hang each one from her bedroom ceiling using some of her Dad's fishing line. She excitedly explained that, as she'd "do" each thing, she'd pluck it from her ceiling and tape it to her bedroom door! *That young lady is going places – she has way too many things to do to allow alcohol, drugs, sex, etc. to getting in the way!*

Research clearly shows that those who write their goals down and make them visible, attain and accomplish much more in their lives. Plan now to do the parent-teen interactive activities regarding goal-setting in chapter 11. As you assist your pre-teen in writing their specific goals, keep in mind this simple acronym to help you more effectively write their goals in a smart (S.M.A.R.T) way.

SMART GOAL PROCESS

Specific – A specific goal has a much greater chance of being accomplished than a general goal. To set a specific goal you must answer the six "W" questions:

Who: Who is involved?
What: What do I want to accomplish?
Where: Identify a location.
When: Establish a time frame.
Which: Identify requirements and constraints.
Why: Specify reasons, a purpose or benefits of accomplishing the goal.

Measurable – Establish concrete criteria for measuring progress toward the attainment of each goal you set. To determine if your goal is measurable, ask questions such as: How much? How many? How will I know when it is accomplished?

Attainable/Action-oriented – When you identify goals that are most important to you, you begin to figure out ways you can make them come true through intentional action. You develop the attitudes, abilities, skills, and financial capacity to achieve them.

Realistic – To be realistic, a goal must represent an objective toward which you are both *willing* and *able* to work. A goal can be both high and realistic; you are the only one who can decide just how high your goal should be.

Timely – A goal should be grounded within a time frame. With no time frame tied to it there's no sense of urgency.

Goal Setting (S.M.A.R.T.)

Specific: Do you know, with all the details, what you want to accomplish?

Measurable: Are you able to assess your progress?

Attainable/Action-oriented: Is your goal within your reach given your current situation? Is there a "do" piece?

Relevant: Is your goal relevant to your purpose in life?

Time-Sensitive: What is the specific time, day, week, month or year for completing your goal?

When brainstorming and writing your respective goals with your pre-teen, keep the following considerations in mind:

- **Think about your priorities in life.**
- **Think about the values you believe in.**
- **Know what you would like to do or be.**
- **Know why you want to choose that goal.**
- **Set realistic and manageable goals.**
- **Be flexible with your goal attainment.**
- **Break a large goal into smaller pieces – small steps are better than no steps!**
- **Secure someone to be your encourager, advisor, listener and evaluator.**
- **Work around roadblocks.**
- **Don't be afraid to fail.**

Writing a bucket list can be invigorating, fun and rewarding. If you are unfamiliar with what a bucket list is, it is a list of things you want to do, experiences you'd like to have, places you'd like to go to, etc. before you die or "kick the bucket." I challenge you as a parent to write your bucket list. I also challenge you to write a joint bucket list (I call it an "Our Bucket List") with your spouse or significant other. Share your lists with your pre-teen to encourage them to begin writing their own. Write a bucket list together with your pre-teen as well. Having plans gives hope. Hope seeps into your attitude and work ethic. Anticipation is half of the fun of having achieved a goal.

Pre-teens and teenagers who have specific attainable goals, written and daily visible, are constantly reminded of where they need to go and what they need to do. I expect great things to happen as you do the interactive activity in chapter 11. It allows you and your pre-teen to identify not only their goals but some of the things that could interfere with the attainment of their goals and bucket list. **This truly empowers them!**

R-E-S-P-E-C-T

Chapter 6

Understanding "Healthy" and "Unhealthy" Teen Relationships

Parents need to know what constitutes a healthy teen relationship before they can effectively talk to their pre-teens about them. This important chapter will help you know what to discuss with your pre-teen about future relationships. We want our children to experience strong and healthy relationships. Nothing is more important than having your pre-teens know what to look for and strive for in a relationship. Without a doubt success and happiness are a direct result of having healthy relationships. Teen relationships have often been established before parents and the child have discussed their importance. Quite often then, it's too late to avoid the negative consequences of a bad choice of companionship. Early conversations with your pre-teen about forming healthy relationships will save a lot of eventual heartaches.

We need to begin by looking at what constitutes a healthy teen relationship. In my many years of working with pre-teens and teens in the classroom and at youth trainings and conferences, a major goal has been to be a very good listener. I have heard what adolescents have said regarding good, solid relationships. I have also heard them describe the bad relationships they found themselves in. The most important thing I have learned through my listening is that relationships are paramount to pre-teens and teens – period! We all can remember where, in the scheme of our values, our relationships stood when we were the age of our pre-teens and teens. Right at or near the top, nothing else really mattered: parents, school, work, etc.

This is why teens that find themselves in unhealthy relationships often resort to alcohol, drugs, sexual activity, not eating, depressive thoughts and maybe even suicide. They lack the positive coping skills needed to deal with the situation they are in. A perceptive parent can see the devastation in their eyes when their cherished relationship has become dysfunctional or has been lost. It is important to understand your child's confusion and hopelessness before you talk to them, whether the lost or troubled relationship they are grieving is a platonic (non-sexual) friendship, and opposite sex relationship or a same sex friendship.

According to Teen Research Unlimited, young people spend a great deal of time thinking about, talking about, and being in romantic relationships.[1] Yet, adults typically dismiss adolescent dating relationships as superficial. Young people see it differently: half of all teens report having been in a dating relationship and nearly one-third of all teens said they have been in a serious relationship.[2] The quality of adolescent romantic relationships can have long lasting effects on self-esteem and shape personal values regarding romance, intimate relationships and sexuality.[3] Romantic relationships become increasingly significant in the lives of young people as they move from early to late adolescence. Although dating may not have begun in early adolescence (ages 10-14), most youth are nonetheless preoccupied with romantic issues. Youths at this time spend significant amounts of time in mixed-gender groups intensifying their romantic interests and may possibly develop romantic relationships.[4] The risks associated with adolescent romantic relationships can be minimized by helping young people develop skills that support healthy relationships.[5]

Youth don't automatically know what constitutes right and wrong behavior within relationships. Without a clear understanding of what makes a healthy relationship, teens are likely to put up with unhealthy behaviors, putting themselves at risk of many unwanted consequences. Teens *have to be taught* the characteristics of healthy relationships, how to differentiate a healthy relationship from an unhealthy one, and how to get help if they find themselves "caught" in an unhealthy relationship. Here is where you come in as proactive parents practicing good parenting!

---

1. Furman, W. (2002) The emerging field of adolescent romantic relationships. *Current Directives in Psychological Science* 11(5), 177-180.
2. Teenage Research Unlimited *(2006). Teen Relationship Abuse Survey.* Liz Claiborne Inc. Retrieved June 29, 2007 from www.loveisnotabuse.com.
3. Barber, B. & Eccles, J. (2003) The joy of romance: Healthy adolescent relationships as an educational agenda. In P. Florsheim (Ed.), *Adolescent romantic relations and sexual behavior: theory, research and practical implications.* Mahwah, NJ. Lawrence Erlbaum Associates.
4. Connolly, J., Craig W., Goldberg, A., & Pepler, D. (2004) Mixed gender groups, dating, and romantic relationships in early adolescence. *Journal of Research on Adolescence, 14(2), 185-207.*
5. Manning, W.D., Giordano, P.C., Longmore, M.A., & Flanigan, C.M. (2206) Adolescent dating relationships and the management of sexual risk. Paper presented at the annual meeting of Population Association of America.

Ingredients of Healthy Relationships

What follows below is the top 20 components that young people have told me that, in their view, constitutes healthy teenage relationships.

1. ***Open communication***—teens felt they needed to feel comfortable talking with the person they liked. They felt they needed the skill to be able to communicate easily with someone whom they like, admire or want a relationship with.
2. ***Balance***—teens wanted a balance of giving and receiving: not all one-sided. Those of my vintage will remember that we use to refer to it as "double-dutch treat."
3. ***Compassion***—teens liked to be in a relationship with those who were empathetic and are willing to share their feelings in constructive ways.
4. ***Honesty***—dishonesty was one of the most common factors that made naïve, simple and even healthy relationships turn sour. Teens want honesty to be paramount although, as we know, for a lot of reasons, immature pre-teens and teens are not invariably honest in their dealings with their parents or their peers.
5. ***Respect***—teens knew they had to respect themselves (which they recognize is quite difficult) and that they should show the same respect for the person they like by not pressuring them to smoke, drink, be sexually active, etc.
6. ***Conflict resolution***—teens mentioned that they hated it when they couldn't resolve their conflicts very well. They admired their peers who were mature enough to talk out their differences and maybe even agree to disagree. They hated shouting matches and being given the silent treatment.
7. ***Ability to just be themselves***—teen shared that they appreciated it when they could *just be themselves* the majority of their time together with the other person in the relationship.
8. ***Power***—teens disliked it when one of the parties in a relationship had the power, made all the plans and decisions, dominated the conversation and made the other feel "inferior."
9. ***Fun/Humor***—teens, like most adults, valued others in a relationship who could just let loose, have fun and laugh about most anything appropriate.
10. ***Forgiveness***—teens shared that they appreciated the readiness of a friend to "ask for forgiveness" when they mess up either intentionally or unintentionally.
11. ***Trust/Jealousy factor***—this was very critical to most teens I talked to. They felt there had to be ways to build trust on a regular basis so that the "jealousy factor" didn't begin to "infect" the relationship
12. ***Respect for sexual limits***—teens liked it when their partner had the will power to respect their "sexual limits." I'll address more about this issue in the next chapter

(chapter 7). They stated they liked being appropriately kissed/ hugged/caressed but wanted their pre-determined sexual limits to be respected

13. ***No time constraints –"if it's meant to be, it'll be"***—teens didn't like being "locked in" to relationships "forever" in their words. They wanted a mutual understanding that, in most cases, the relationship will end, and that's OK.

14. ***Accepting of differences***—most teens thought it was critical to be able to accept each other's differences, no matter what! Talents, strengths and weaknesses all had to be accepted in a mature relationship.

15. ***Public and Private behaviors***—most teens did not like P.D.A.s (public displays of affection). Most wanted to be treated with overall respect both while in private or when out in public. That included no gross sarcasm or intentional put downs.

16. ***Knowledge of infatuation vs. love***—this is where the "rubber meets the road." Most teens were not able to understand the difference between these two terms and many, many, many relationships self-destruct because of this issue alone. Parents, it is extremely important to make sure your teen knows the difference. I would highly recommend you read a book written by Dr. Ray Short entitled, "Sex, Love or Infatuation" to really understand their differences.

17. ***Ability to control hormones***—some teens appreciated the importance of controlling their urges. Those who didn't were likely to become sexually active. The pressure to engage in sexual activity either turns the relationship into a sexual one or completely ends it, depending on the expectations and maturity level of the teens involved.

18. ***Drug and or alcohol usage***—this was one of the top five concerns, especially if one, but not the other, was a user. When both were using drugs or alcohol it invariably resulted in an unhealthy relationship.

19. ***Parental respect***—believe it or not, a lot of teens I talked to base their eventual decisions in a relationship on the respect they have for their parents! This could be good OR bad depending on the model their parents presented to them!

20. ***Appreciation for each other's short- and long-term goals***—teens want their partner in a relationship to respect and support them in reaching their short- and long-term goals.

I think you will agree that this is a pretty impressive list of desirable components to insure a healthy relationship. Many of these aspirations were expressed by teens that ended a relationship because it didn't have one or several of these components. As a parent, be ready to discuss these components with your pre-teen or teen, especially before using the interactive activity, "Are You Ready?" in chapter 10.

The POWERS to be....!

Chapter 7

Understanding the sexual relationship continuum

As you know, relationships can be healthy or unhealthy. "Sex" when introduced into a teen relationship often weakens and eventually destroys it.

To begin, I need to define several terms I will be using in this chapter. First, most people use the word "sex" inappropriately. *"Sex"* refers to your gender – male or female! So, if you asked your pre-teen, "are you having sex?" they could respond by saying, "yes, I am; I am enjoying being a male (or female)!" *"Sexual activity"* is another ambiguous term that needs to be clarified. It describes any behavior that stimulates another person – physically or emotionally. This could be something as simple as caressing an arm or casual kissing. It also includes sexual actions like heavy petting and "going all the way" or engaging in sexual intercourse. *"Sexual intercourse"* or coitus then, is the act by which humans reproduce. Oral and anal intercourse doesn't result in reproduction but may have serious health effects.

As parents, it is important to understand that teens are confronted with a continuum of appropriate and inappropriate behaviors as they build their relationships. It is critical that parents and teens understand the role that "hormones" play in teenage relationships. I believe that it is just as dangerous to "be under the influence" of hormones as it is to be under the influence of alcohol and/or drugs! And yes, many teens make decisions under the influence of BOTH. Sexual arousal clouds their ability to reason clearly and look ahead to see the consequences of their actions. Many intelligent, talented, well-meaning teens with goals and aspirations have made unwise decisions that have negatively influenced their lives. Damaged reputations, unwanted pregnancies, early marriages, sexually transmitted infections (S.T.I.s), as well as unrealized educational goals are just a few of the life-changing consequences of teenage sexual activity.

This chapter will help you understand a relationship continuum that ranges from simple attraction to sexual intercourse. After you understand it, it is critical that you share what you know with your pre-teen or teenager. The following sections describe how relationships begin during the pre-teen or teen years and how they could end badly without the proper knowledge, boundaries and communication. Let's start by looking at the relationship as stages. Heterosexual relationships can start very simply and end up very involved.

Relationship Continuum Involving Sexual Activity

<<<DANGER ZONE>>>

Stage 1	Stage 2	Stage 3	Stage 4
Attraction	Dating/"Going Out"/"Hooking up"	Physical Intimacy	Sexual Intercourse

Stage 1 – Attraction

Most pre-teen relationships start pretty simply. Back "in the day" pre-teens often started the process by passing notes to someone they liked. You remember, "check the box if you like me" and "check the box if you want to 'go out.'" It makes us smile as we look back on those behaviors. In that attraction stage, a smile from someone you admired could make you feel warm all over! Another early pre-teen ritual was "sending in the troops" which included sending all of your friends to the one you liked to ask if they like you!

Are those memories coming back? This stage also included talking on the phone (it would be texting today) and maybe hanging out in safe groups of mixed gender kids but always trying to get in the same group with that person you felt was special. Few problems with the attraction stage in a relationship back then and/or today.

Stage 2 – Dating/Going out/Hooking up

When teens begin dating, they assume that they are "going out" or "going together" and there is usually an understanding that they should be true to each other and not date anyone else. In many cases today that has changed with the social freedom of having "friends with benefits." "Friends with benefits" describes a temporary, and sometimes serial, relationship in which it is understood that sexual "benefits" will be granted during the date with no long-term expectations or obligations.

Needless to say, such arrangements are unhealthy and dangerous. Fortunately, most teens in this second stage restrict themselves to holding hands, may briefly kiss and hug each other, go out to movies or athletic events, buy each other gifts and just hang out watching television. Responsible teens in a healthy relationship usually can behave responsibly in this stage when they are alone, but are also comfortable when they are in social situations with adults. Mature teens that understand and adhere to this continuum can thrive here and have enjoyable and healthy relationships.

Stage 3---The "Danger Zone"

Unfortunately, teens sometimes define their relationships by the amount of sexual activity they engage in. I call this stage the "physical intimacy stage." Here's where we lose many of our teens to the power of hormones! If sexual advances are made by one or both parties in a relationship, they can elicit dangerous hormonal explosions. I truly believe that being under the influence of hormones can be just as dangerous as being under the influence of alcohol and/or drugs. And yes, many teens are often under the influence of both, making it doubly dangerous. It is in this stage that the danger zone begins. Teens may "french kiss" in lieu of a normal appropriate kiss. They may "pet," "paw," or caress each other in areas of privacy. They may fondle each other. You may have your understanding of fondling, but I have my own definition. Fondling is touching another person's body in a place where they are "supposed to have" two layers of clothing!

I was explaining this to my daughter when she was about 12 years of age. After thinking a bit, she smiled, looked up at me and said, "Dad, I won't let any guy touch my feet." I immediately began to laugh hysterically and told her I wasn't talking about *there* but other more private areas on your body!

Some teens acquire hickeys at a variety of places on their bodies during this stage. Others "practice" oral sex believing that it is much safer than sexual intercourse. What they don't understand is that they can contract S.T.I.s in their mouths, throats and eyes. And, for all of the viral S.T.I.s there is no cure! Once a young person acquires them, they remain infected for life!

The final danger of this stage of intimacy is that normal mores are forgotten, consequences are ignored, emotions become the engine of the relationship, and the couple skips right into stage four. Now if they add alcohol or drugs into the scenario, it greatly speeds up the continuum and almost guarantees that the relationship will skip to the next stage.

Stage 4-Sexual intercourse

I have never met a teen who woke up in the morning and said, "I can't wait to get pregnant (or get someone pregnant) tonight!" Not one. I believe sexually-active teens are trying to fulfill their basic inherent needs of love, touch and acceptance by getting into stage three of the relationship. Often, they simply don't know of any other healthy ways to get those needs met. Many very intelligent, good kids get drawn in by the power of hormones, alcohol or drugs and the euphoria of their newly established relationship. Most teens enter stage four drunk, high or heavily under the influence of hormones and end up "going all the way" and engaging in sexual intercourse. In most cases, once "experienced," they will continue to engage in sexual intercourse, especially if there were no major consequences the first few times. Teen pregnancies, S.T.I.s and many other unwanted consequences await them.

Your goal as parents or concerned mentors is to make sure your pre-teen and/or teen knows this continuum before they enter any relationship. Your child needs to know the following:

1. Understand the continuum and be able to say where they are at any given time in a relationship.
2. Be able to talk to their partner while they are drug free, sober and unemotional about their sexual limits.
3. Make their sexual limits known to their partner before stage three!
4. Understand the dangerous impact that alcohol, drugs and hormones have on a relationship.

According to the Kaiser Family Foundation, over the last ten years the percentage of high school students who reported having sexual intercourse has declined. They also report that young men and young women in all four grades of high school were more likely to stay abstinent if they knew their mothers disapproved of premarital sex. They also found that girls in eighth and ninth grades were more likely to avoid sex if their mothers talked regularly with their friends' parents. I maintain that the likelihood of raising teenagers who will delay sexual activity would be even greater if caring adults regularly communicate with them on these sensitive issues.

Parents, once again I urge you to begin healthy conversations with your pre-teen or teen about this sexual continuum. Interactive activities involving this topic can be found in chapter 11. One of the activities will allow you and your teen to specifically discuss situations where hormones may get out of control and what behaviors could occur when that happens. You and your pre-teen will benefit from this discussion and interactive activity.

Remember: Don't Freak, Tweak your Teens…

and EMPOWER them with the right information, the developmental assets and the needed life skills.

What happened…..?

Chapter 8

The many consequences of teenage sexual activity

When I ask teens, "What would be your biggest and most immediate worry if you had sexual intercourse?" they all quickly respond, "My biggest concern would be 'did I get pregnant?' (or 'did I get her pregnant?')." I point out that pregnancy is just one of the 30 mental, social, financial and physical consequences most teens fail to consider when they choose to be sexually active. Most teens only think of the physical consequence – a pregnancy – and most believe, of course, it will *never* happen to them!

The consequences I share in this chapter have not come from any single resource but from teens all over the country. They have been reported by teens, all of whom were, or presently are, sexually active. They come from treatment centers, juvenile detention institutions, youth groups, support groups, leadership groups, and high school classroom discussions. They powerfully press home the fact that there are many consequences of teenage sexual activity other than pregnancy.

The lists below are arranged in specific categories of Mental/Emotional, Social, Financial and Physical consequences. Realize that many of them interconnect and have multiple outcomes!

Basically guys are subject to the same Mental/Emotional, Social, Financial and Physical consequences as the girls, **BUT THEY DON'T GET PREGNANT!** So, quite naturally, guys tend to take more risks. Girls need to know this.

As I travel the country, I find that more and more young men are choosing abstinence and are very proud of their decision. I often ask teen groups this question: Do you think we'd have fewer unwanted teen pregnancies if guys could get pregnant? There usually is a vigorous nodding of all their heads!

Parents, again it is crucial that you communicate these *many* other consequences to your pre-teen or teenager before they enter any relationship. I cannot stress enough how important it is for you to mutually work on the interactive activities found in chapter 11 regarding the consequences of teen sexual activity. Use these activities not only to share the many unconsidered consequences with your teen, but to discuss their options – abstinence until they are in a committed relationship being one option.

Mental/Emotional:

- Feel used/abused
- Feel guilty
- Feel confused
- Feel "empty"
- Feel afraid/scared
- Feel anxious/worried/nervous
- Feel depressed
- Develop a lower self-esteem
- Begin to lose self-confidence
- Begin to think that other unhealthy behaviors are okay

Social:

- Loss of close friends who aren't sexually-active
- Reputation is damaged
- Future relationships may be affected
- Loss of trust with parents
- Increase in popularity with sexually-active peers
- Decrease in popularity with non-sexually-active peers

Financial:

- Possible pregnancy testing
- S.T.I. testing
- Doctor check-ups
- Contraception costs
- Abortion costs
- Birthing costs
- Alimony/child support for 18 years (NOTE: It has been estimated that it costs approximately $245,340 to raise a child to the age of 18 in today's economy!)

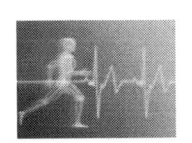

Physical:

(NOTE: I share this category last since most teens think of these first!)

- May get an S.T.I.
- May develop cervical cancer from acquiring the S.T. I. – HPV (human papilloma virus)
- May have to have a hysterectomy (removal of uterus) and be unable to have children in the future.
- May get AIDS
- May get physically addicted to alcohol/drugs and have to deal with the mental consequences of those addictions
- May get stretch-marks on their body as a teen if they give birth to a child
- Lastly, they may get pregnant!

Toolbox of Life Skills

Chapter 9

Critical life skills your pre-teen needs to know and utilize to live well and develop healthy relationships

**Remember that pre-teen empowerment formula
I shared with you in Chapter 4?**

Knowledge + life skills + assets = Empowered Pre-teen

In this chapter I'll be sharing the critically important life skills that all teens need to know and to utilize so they will make decisions that will lead to a healthy and successful life. These skills will empower and guide them in developing future relationships. The research is clear showing that knowledge alone does not guarantee that teens will make better or healthier decisions. On the other hand, I believe that a blend of specific knowledge, critical assets, and the following seven life skills allows them to exert positive control over the majority of the decisions they will be making. These are the life skills that are essential to your pre-teen's successful development. Although I think these skills can be taught by you to your pre-teens, I believe that every K-12 school system should be teaching them somewhere within the structure of their curriculum.

- **Assertiveness skill**
- **Quick and healthy decision-making skill**
- **Problem-solving skill**
- **Communication skill**
- **Active-listening skill**
- **"Know" skill**
- **Care-frontation skill**

Assertiveness skill

This life skill allows a teen to effectively stand up for what they believe is healthy, legal and safe and state their position in a calm, caring, respectful manner while feeling in control.

Specific sub-skills your pre-teen needs to have when behaving assertively include:
- Finding a way to begin the conversation with a compliment
- Maintaining immediate but not constant eye contact (although good eye contact)
- Standing in close proximity to the person they are talking to (within 2-4 feet)
- Standing, sitting, or kneeling at same physical level of the person they are communicating with
- Keeping their voice calm
- Maintaining a confident tone to their voice
- Using gracious words – for example, using "please," "would you be so kind," etc.
- Concluding with a "thanks for respecting my wishes…" statement at the end, or simply a "thank you"

Being assertive also means that if pressures continue your pre-teen needs to re-state exactly what they said with no major changes from their initial statement! This is a critical life skill needed to resist bullying, pressure to use alcohol or drugs, or sexual pressures. When you have appropriate opportunities, set up various threatening life scenarios and have your pre-teen explain what they might do *assertively* in those situations.

Quick and healthy decision-making skill

This powerful life skill will help your pre-teen decide upon an appropriate course of action, even when he or she is under pressure to decide quickly.

It has to be used when the pre-teen is NOT under the influence of alcohol, drugs and or hormones. It simply won't be remembered or utilized when under those influences. But if pressure is being put on your pre-teen to use alcohol, drugs, or to yield to the lure of hormones, this skill will help him or her keep their head.

It is used when your pre-teen doesn't have a lot of time to make their decision. This skill, when learned and practiced, can be effectively utilized in 10-15 seconds! When your pre-teen is faced with a decision they have to be able to ask themselves five quick questions within 10-15 seconds. These questions include:

- Is it healthy?
- Is it safe?
- Is it legal?
- Does it respect the wishes of my parents/guardians?
- Does it respect my wishes and the wishes of others?

IF your child answers NO to any one of these questions within those 5-10 seconds, he/she should be assertive and decide not do it. IF they decide to do it, they simply need to understand that they had better be ready for ANY of the consequences that could occur.

Pre-teens can learn this skill fairly easily and, if utilized on a regular basis, it can save them many unnecessary consequences throughout their years of development and beyond.

You can easily see many of these life skills are dependent on each other. For instance, after using the quick and healthy decision-making skill, they'll need to be assertive when stating their decision.

The problem-solving skill

This skill is used when a teen *has time* to think about and consider ALL options.

We all need help solving issues and problems that crop up in our lives. Teens, especially, need to be taught this basic life skill to equip them with the ability to work through and solve their own issues or problems when they don't have, or don't want, anyone else's input. Most teens do not know how to solve problems due to their lack of life experiences so we need to teach them. This skill is designed to make your teen an independent thinker and problem-solver.

The steps in this skill include:

- **Identify the specific issue or problem.**
- **Brainstorm and write down a list of all possible choices.**
- **List the "pros" and "cons" of each possible choice.**
- **Choose one alternative.**
- **Use the quick and healthy decision-making skill to help you decide.**
- **Make a decision.**
- **Evaluate.**

This skill is very powerful and can be used to decide many things like whether or not to continue a relationship, what university to attend, whether or not to attend a party where there'll be underage alcohol or drug use, etc. Teach your pre-teen this skill while using the interactive activity in chapter 11, where you and your pre-teen utilize the skill in a variety of relevant scenarios.

The communication life skill

This life skill can be effectively utilized by both parents and pre-teens. This specific skill enhances communication immensely. It is non-judgmental, non-accusatory and allows both parties to let each other know how they feel and what they want or need. Parents, I challenge you to become competent with this skill and begin using it with your own spouse or significant other before teaching it to your pre-teen. It is sometimes called the "I" formula because it starts with an "I" statement.

Here are the specific steps of the communication life skill:

- **Say the person's name** to secure their attention
- **Say…. "I feel"….**

    Here, one shares an *emotion* they are feeling. Simply share the specific emotions (feelings) that are leading you to communicate with them. Feelings might include anger, frustration, confusion, worry, etc.

- **Next say…. "when"…**

    After the word "when," share what the circumstance is that's causing your feeling. An example here might be, "when I try to keep our home clean and things are just thrown everywhere…."

- **Then say…. "because"…**

    After the word "because," share how it is affecting you. For instance, "I have to spend a lot of my valuable time picking up after everyone…"

- **Next continue the conversation with one of the following:**
    o What I want…
    o What I would like…
    o Would you consider…

    In this step, *specifically* say what you want, need or would like them to consider!

- **Finish the conversation by saying, "Thank you" or just "thanks."**

    Complete the skill using these kind words which simply thanks them ahead of time. This is an important step. I am sure most of you have received a bill in the mail that was due and on the bottom it stated, "thank you for paying your bill on time." I always feel compelled to pay that bill ON TIME! They already thanked me!

This skill is demonstrably more powerful if you keep your voice low, stay calm and collected as you progress through the steps.

Are you beginning to see how this skill may be used effectively by your pre-teen when they want to better communicate with their peers, boyfriend or girlfriend regarding issues of sexual pressure, alcohol or drug use? Can you readily see that your teens need to be assertive and use the quick decision-making skill in order to use this skill to better communicate?

As they say, "Try it, you'll really like it!" Good luck effectively communicating as a family!

The active-listening skill

This life skill takes some practice. Most of us don't listen very well. As a parent you really need to begin paying attention to what your pre-teen or teen is saying and try to sense what they are feeling. When your teen believes they are being *heard*, they are more likely to communicate, compromise and resolve the conflict.

These 3 elements are essential to active listening:

Paraphrasing: intermittently summarizing what was just said, putting it into your own words and re-stating it to the person with whom you are communicating. You can do this intermittently by stating, "so what you're saying is….."

Validating: occasionally questioning what you heard in order to validate your perception of what was said. You can do this by stating, "Did I hear you right when you said…."

Clarifying: again, restating a word, phrase or concept when you are unclear about what you heard. You can do this by stating, "Did you just say, 'next year?' "

Below are 5 guidelines to aid in your active listening:

- **Encourage the person you are listening to** by raising your eyebrows, looking them in their eyes, and tilting your head slightly to show your willingness to truly listen. Do not argue, blame, moralize, judge, accuse, insult or threaten. Above all, DON'T INTERRUPT, AND DON'T COMPLETE THEIR SENTENCES!
- **Stay focused** on what they are saying and the feelings they are revealing.
- **Paraphrase, validate and clarify** when possible. Try not to be thinking of a response as you are listening.
- **Make verbal or non-verbal statements** that suggest acceptance, understanding and appreciation.
- **Allow for some silence before you speak.** It lets the other party know that you are assimilating what they said.

Again, listening is hard work. It is a life skill that most adults need to practice and refine. Work on it with your spouse and/or significant other. Try it with you pre-teen. Know that it will take some time to change your previous ways of "listening." In chapter 11, you will find a specific interactive activity to practice effective listening with your pre-teen. Once again, you will notice that in order to use the previously learned communication skill ("I" formula) you'll need to be able to listen as well. It is no different for your pre-teen as they enter relationships that hopefully will be healthy ones.

The "KNOW" life skill

This is a powerful life skill not known and thus, not used by many teenagers. When President Ronald Reagan took office, his wife, Nancy, initiated an anti-drug-and-alcohol campaign for youth. I vividly remember her making a statement to our country's youth. "Just say no, boys and girls, to alcohol and drugs…." Although I commended her for taking on the issue, I choked back my frustration with her statement. It is not as simple as just saying "no."

Our pre-teens and teens need to KNOW how to say NO. They also need to know and utilize a specific life skill called the "KNOW" skill.

The skill has 2 goals:

- **To allow your youth to say no and still keep their friends**
- **To allow your youth to say no and still have fun**

Most pre-teens and teens that I speak with today say they would say "no" more often if they could say it and still have fun, keep their friends, stay out of trouble and be in control. Many youth say yes because they don't want to lose their friends and they want to have fun – two very important things in their lives when they are between the ages of 11 and 14.

Here are the 4 steps to the KNOW life skill:

- **Think about your decision**
- **State *only one* consequence and repeat it**
- **Share and sell something different**
- **Physically move as you invite your friends to be with you**

Think about your decision:

Step one involves making a quick and healthy decision. The pre-teen or teen should already know this skill. Remember, it is the one where they are to ask themselves the five questions to see if it is healthy, legal, safe, if it would please their parents and if they would feel good about what they were doing? Also remember that this should only take 10-15 seconds. Let your teen know that if they answer no to any one of the five questions, they should not do it. If they make a decision that may be risky and unhealthy, they need to be ready for any of the consequences. Speaking of consequences, if they still want to keep their friends, stay in control, stay out of trouble, and still have fun, they need to proceed to the next step.

State *only one* consequence and repeat it:

Once your pre-teen knows that the pressure is on them to decide and there is possible trouble, yet they still want to keep their friend(s) and have fun, this step follows in the sequence. They need to assertively state *one* realistic, negative consequence. If pressure continues from their friend or peer, they need only to *repeat* the same consequence mentioned before. This is important because each time they repeat the consequence, their friend realizes that they have solidly made up their mind. Teach your teen to respond in a "matter of fact" and confident manner.

Share and sell something different:

If the consequence has been stated several times, your pre-teen needs to then attempt to sell an alternative that is equal to or more inviting than their friend's proposal. If your teen has no viable alternative to offer, they need to skip this step and go right to the final step. But, if they still want to have fun, keep their friends, and stay out of trouble, they need to offer an appealing alternative for their friends or peers to consider. Invite them to do something different that is healthy, legal and safe. If the friends or peers still don't want to buy into the alternative suggestion, your pre-teen should immediately go to the final step.

Physically move as you invite your friends to be with you:

This is the most powerful step and allows teens to refuse effectively. Most teens sit and debate the choices and alternatives until they get broken down. Here, your pre-teen actually starts to walk away (if they can in the situation) and states what they would like their friend or their peers to do, inviting them one more time. Now the power is with your pre-teen since the others pressuring him/her are forced to make a decision one way or another.

This skill, when used, effectively can give your child a very unique opportunity to say "no" and still keep their friends and have fun! Enjoy practicing this life skill in one of the interactive activities within chapter 11.

<u>Knowing</u> is having the knowledge and the skill to refuse!

The care-frontation life skill

Do you have anyone in your life that you are concerned about because of specific behaviors you see and hear about, but you don't know how to approach them or don't know what to say to them? Most of us do. So do our pre-teens. They know which of their peers are sexually active or using alcohol or drugs. This skill is useful for both parents and pre-teens. It allows anyone who may be concerned about another person's behavior to "confront" them in a caring, non-threatening, and non-judgmental manner.

The steps for the care-frontation life skill are:

- Say their name
- Say, "I care/love/am concerned..."
- Say, "I see..."
- Say, "I feel..."
- Listen...
- Say, "I want..."
- Say, "I will..."

Say their name:

To begin using this powerful skill, one has to state the name of the person they are talking to and are concerned about. This should be done assertively and in a low, caring, comforting tone of voice.

Say, "I care/love/am concerned..."

This step is a very important one. It allows the person who is concerned to state *why* they want to communicate with the other person. Depending on the relationship, the user of the skill states whether they "care about" or "love" the person they are confronting. If neither of these phrases seems appropriate one could say something as simple as "you've been a great friend of mine for a long time and I am concerned about you..." This often deflates any negative feelings that can be present in a "confrontation." A short delay or brief time of silence after this statement can be very powerful.

Say, "I see..."

Here one tells all the personally observed behaviors and known hard facts that you are concerned about. Notice I mentioned personally observed behaviors and hard facts. Share *only* behaviors, concerns and facts that they cannot deny or argue with. Avoid saying what you've heard or what others may think, which often opens the door for the person you are confronting to deny those happenings. Share as many personally observable behaviors and known hard facts as you can.

Say, "I feel..."

Next, share an emotion or emotions you are feeling. "when you"…..is NOT a feeling. A feeling is an emotion. Tune into what you are truly feeling and share it honestly. When done, open the door for communication by simply remaining quiet and not talking. Remember, silence is golden. Most people are uncomfortable with silence, even when they are confronted in a caring way.

Listen…

This actually is the hardest step. Allow for silence. Usually people check into their feelings and are thinking during this time! Most people want to immediately offer advice here – refrain. Allow the door to open so they begin to share.

Say, "I want…"

When you are done listening to them, state what you want. Be brutally honest here but continue speaking in a caring, non-judgmental, non-threatening manner.

Say, "I will…"

Tell them explicitly what you are willing to do to help them. Be specific and always follow through. This is what separates a normal confrontation from this "care-frontation" life skill.

Use this skill in your relationships before you teach it to your pre-teen. Find out how powerful this skill really is! It is most effective when done face-to-face or on the phone. But it can be partially accomplished by writing it in a card or letter or by texting your concerns.

I am excited for you to learn this skill yourself but also for you to teach it to your pre-teen. They can then add it to their "toolbox" with the many other critical life skills you are teaching them.

Encourage use of all these skills as often as possible! After all, they are important tools that need to be in your child's LIFE toolbox!

Where are my keys....?
Chapter 10
Keys to dating and experiencing healthy relationships

All parents need to be clear in their own mind regarding their expectations of their pre-teen's or teen's behaviors in a relationship *before* they communicate with them. This chapter will present the keys you need to know about and be prepared to teach your pre-teen or teen. There are interactive activities in chapter 11 that both you and your pre-teen can work on relating to dating expectations.

But first, I need to make a general statement regarding dating. I have seen, heard and dealt with heartache from teens who started dating too early. These experiences have convinced me that *group dating* should be an initial priority. So establish the expectation with your pre-teen that they will begin their dating relationships by socializing in groups of teens from both sexes. In a group they can see what they like or dislike about various opposite sex friends without having to make any long-term commitments. It allows them the practice of being with others they find attractive in a non-threatening and safe environment. "Dating" or "going out" too early risks jealousies, dishonesty, hurt feelings and sometimes damaged reputations.

However, when you and your pre-teen decide it is appropriate for them to have a more personal relationship and begin to date and/or go out, there are several keys that will help to make the experience a healthy and rewarding one.

20 keys for healthy dating relationships: (For pre-teens/teens)

1. You need to understand that dating is a privilege, not a right. You have to build enough trust with your parent to be allowed this privilege. Waiting a bit to "officially" date might just save you a lot of headaches and heartaches!
2. You have to be responsible in what you do with your body and mind.
3. You have to be able to communicate effectively with your parents and your special friend.
4. You need to know and use the life skills that allow for making healthy, legal and safe decisions. Use the "toolbox" of life skills needed to insure happy and healthy relationships.
5. You need to know and understand the "sexual activity" relationship continuum.
6. You need to respect yourself and others. Treat your date with 100% respect – their mind, their body and their spirit.
7. You need to be aware of and convinced of your values before entering a relationship.
8. You should not go on a date just to please others.
9. You should never let your emotions control your behaviors. Truly understand and respect the power of hormones.
10. You should know and respect the fact that alcohol and drug use will eventually cause problems in nearly all relationships.
11. You should never ride with a date who is driving under the influence – NEVER! Always have a back-up plan for a non-drinking friend or your parents to pick you up in the event your date begins to drink or use drugs.
12. While on a date, continually ask yourself — "would my parents/guardians be proud of my behaviors right now?"
13. You should avoid spending long periods of time alone with your date.
14. You should insist on being in areas during your date where you can safely leave if you decide you need to do so.
15. You should remind yourself of your goals in life when you are pressured to use alcohol, drugs or engage in sexual activities.
16. If you ever feel "trapped" in a relationship break it off as early as possible.

17. You need to know that most relationships are temporary, and the one you are currently in may someday end.
18. You should learn things from each relationship you engage in.
19. You need to know the differences between love and infatuation.
20. You need to communicate with your parents/guardians about your relationship with the person you like.

Parents, it is critical to share these keys with your pre-teen *before their first date*, especially before important events like prom or homecoming. Often, when the date has spent money for attire, flowers and meals, both partners can begin to think they "owe" the other person more than a mere evening of togetherness. Generally the best time to discuss these issues and talk about these keys is between the ages of twelve to fourteen – 7th, 8th or 9th grade. Understanding these keys is a huge step towards providing them an opportunity to enjoy many sound, healthy relationships to come.

Give your teen the keys to healthy relationships before you give them the keys to the family car!

So Happy Together.....!

Chapter 11

Let's work together.......time to interact.

This chapter introduces you to a variety of interactive activities. Take the information you have learned from chapters 1-10 and use it to effectively communicate and comfortably interact with your pre-teen. Your pre-teen will soon be forming romantic relationships and facing the big decisions discussed in chapters 1 - 10.

TO PARENTS:

Strong relationships are built on trust. Parent-teen relationships require a solid foundation of trust allowing parents and their child to discuss important issues. This interactive working section of the book is where the "rubber meets the road" and you begin to use your newly acquired knowledge, assets and life skills with your pre-teen. It is now time to plan regular interactive activity times with your pre-teen to discuss the issues that will impact their future relationships.

In specific cases, when trust between parent and pre-teen is lacking, these activities could be worked on and completed with a respected non-parent mentor, but both parent and teen lose something valuable when that is done. These activities offer you and your pre-teen many hours of rewarding and productive interaction.

TO TEENS:

You are beginning to fill your days with more and more life-shaping experiences and taking on greater and greater responsibilities. You will soon face, if you have not already, several important life decisions that will challenge your present values and loyalties. Decisions such as whether to use alcohol or drugs, whether to engage in sexual activity, or how to cope with depression are just a few of the issues facing you and your peers.

You are extremely fortunate to have a parent that is willing to take the time to interact with you, share sound information with you, and assist you in developing life skills that will give you a big advantage in life! This "chapter" in your life can be a fantastic one. This parent-teen interactive guide was designed to assist you and your parents as you discuss interesting, and sometimes difficult issues. These times of interaction will build mutual trust and help you develop open communication. The activities you and your parents are about to engage in will allow you to be a more *powerful* teen with the maturity and skills to make informed decisions leading to healthy and rewarding relationships.

This is your opportunity to avoid the irresponsible behaviors many teens engage in and grow into the responsible young adult you and your parents want you to become.

PARENTS AND PRE-TEEN

Here is a list of interactive activities you will work on together. Enjoy the opportunity to communicate, grow and build trust. Many parents and their pre-teens will *never* have this opportunity!

1. Definitions Missing….
2. Assessing my Assets
3. Life Decisions with Impact
4. Goals, Wishes and Dreams
5. Creating Healthy Teen Relationships
6. Consequences, consequences, consequences… pre- and teen-age sexual relationships
7. Hormones Out of Control
8. Pros and Cons of Abstinence
9. Life Skills: My Toolbox for Life!
10. Am I Ready?
11. Mutual Expectation
12. Parent – Pre-teen Contracts

Conclusion . . . or Beginning?

I believe the knowledge you have gained from reading this book and the time spent interacting with your pre-teen will be invaluable to you and your pre-teen! It is my hope and mission that pre-teens develop into wholesome young men and women that enjoy many healthy relationships! Enjoy watching your child grow and develop with the necessary knowledge, life skills and assets that will set them up for a life of health, happiness and success. Remember you are "tweaking," not freaking…and empowering your pre-teen for many opportunities to have a rewarding life! Keep on caring no matter what. I live by these wise words, spoken first by Theodore Roosevelt:

"NOBODY CARES HOW MUCH YOU KNOW UNTIL THEY KNOW HOW MUCH YOU CARE"

ENJOY the experience of preparing your pre-teen for a healthy life and many healthy relationships as well!

It's JUST the BEGINNING!

Interactive Activity #1

"Definitions missing....!"

Parents, this activity can be easily facilitated by writing all of these words and concepts on separate sheets of paper and putting them in a jar. Once in the jar, schedule a time that's convenient for both of you and pick one or two words or concepts to discuss and/or define.

OR

Use this worksheet of words and concepts, going through them one by one, in the order I have them listed. Using this strategy might be a bit more appealing since I have arranged them in a specific order, putting less threatening topics first, to aid in establishing a comfort level as you work together through the list. Use them when you judge your pre-teen is mentally, physically and/or emotionally ready to discuss each particular subject.

Also, since both parent and pre-teen will have the words and concepts ahead of time, each can prepare their thoughts before communication begins!

"to educate,"
(from

Remember our mathematical formula for success?

<u>KNOWLEDGE</u> + ASSETS + LIFE SKILLS = EMPOWERED TEEN!

Fair Use: Copies of this activity may be made for personal use. No mass production for distribution, or alteration of this activity is permitted without prior consent of the author.

Terms and concepts to discuss and define:

- Respect for self
- Underage alcohol use
- Drug use
- Smoking
- Chewing tobacco
- Consequences
- Being accountable
- Responsibilities in healthy relationships
- My faith's role in establishing the values needed in healthy relationships
- Respect for someone of "interest"
- Empathy
- Bullying
- Eating disorders
- Self-injury or cutting
- Depression/suicide
- Coping
- Life skills needed to make good decisions and develop healthy relationships
- Commitment
- Boundaries

- Death or loss
- Infatuation
- Love
- Dignity
- Will power/Restraint
- Dangers of unhealthy relationships
- "Sex" vs. "Sexual activity" vs. "Sexual intercourse"
- Sexual activity in a teen relationship
- Consequences of early sexual activity
- Goals and unwanted teen pregnancies
- Contraception
- "Safe-" vs. "Safer-" sex (There is no such thing as "safe sex"; with contraception it may be "safer".)
- Abstinence/Virginity
- Respecting sexual differences
- Building a mutual trust between parent-teen
- Pre-teen or teen expectations of parent

Add any other topics that you decide to discuss – "the sky is the limit."

Fair Use: Copies of this activity may be made for personal use. No mass production for distribution, or alteration of this activity is permitted without prior consent of the author.

Interactive Activity #2
Assessing my Assets....!

Parent:

As you now know, developmental assets are a set of heavily researched "building blocks" needed to insure your teen the opportunities for a happy, healthy and successful life. You may want to discuss what you have learned about developmental assets with your pre-teen before this activity. This interactive activity will allow you and your pre-teen to assess the assets at your, and your pre-teen's disposal. Complete the Parent Checklist and use it as the basis of a discussion with your pre-teen about ways to acquire the assets needed and to strengthen those already in his or her possession. If the number of assets is found to be high, you nonetheless need to discuss a plan to maintain those assets as the research shows that the assets fluctuate over time and may even decrease as the child moves into his or her teen years or beyond.

Pre-teen:

Developmental assets are a heavily researched set of "building blocks" needed to insure you the opportunity for a happy, healthy and successful life. This interactive activity will allow you and your parents to assess the number of assets already at your disposal and those you need to acquire. By completing the Pre-teen Checklist you will be able to determine how many developmental assets you have at your disposal. The closer you are to having all 40 assets, the greater will be your chance of enjoying a healthy, happy and successful life. The fewer you have, the more you need to create an intentional plan to secure them.

Both:

After both parties have completed their checklist set aside a time to discuss each asset, those the pre-teen has, and those he or she does not have. Create a plan for acquiring and securing the assets needed. Even if the number of assets is found to be high, it is important to discuss a plan to maintain those assets as the research is clear that the assets fluctuate and sometimes decrease as the pre-teen becomes a teenager and later a young adult. When done, compare and discuss answers and finalize your plan using the "Parent-teen Asset Contract."

Fair Use: Copies of this activity may be made for personal use. No mass production for distribution, or alteration of this activity is permitted without prior consent of the author.

PRE-TEEN
Asset Assessment Checklist

1. **Family support** — Your family life provides high levels of love and support.

    ___ Yes ___ No

2. **Positive family communication** — You communicate positively with your parents/guardians. You feel comfortable seeking advice and counsel from them.

    ___ Yes ___ No

3. **Other adult relationships** — You receive support from adults other than your parents/guardians.

    ___ Yes ___ No

4. **Caring neighborhood** — You experience caring neighbors.

    ___ Yes ___ No

5. **Caring school climate** — Your relationships with teachers and peers provide a caring, encouraging environment.

    ___ Yes ___ No

6. **Parent involvement in schooling** — Your parents are actively involved in helping you succeed in school.

    ___ Yes ___ No

7. **Community values youth** — You feel valued and appreciated by adults in your community.

    ___ Yes ___ No

8. **Children as resources** — You are included in decisions at home and in the community.

    ___ Yes ___ No

9. **Service to others** — You have opportunities to help others in your community.

    ___ Yes ___ No

10. **Safety** — You feel safe at home, at school, and in your neighborhood.

    ___ Yes ___ No

Fair Use: Copies of this activity may be made for personal use. No mass production for distribution, or alteration of this activity is permitted without prior consent of the author.

11. Family boundaries — Your family has clear and consistent rules and consequences and monitors your whereabouts.

___ Yes ___ No

12. School boundaries — Your school provides clear rules and consequences.

___ Yes ___ No

13. Neighborhood boundaries — Your neighbors take responsibility for monitoring your behavior if parents/guardians aren't available.

___ Yes ___ No

14. Adult role models — Your parents and other adults in your family, as well as nonfamily adults, model positive, responsible behavior.

___ Yes ___ No

15. Friends — Your closest friends model positive, responsible behavior.

___ Yes ___ No

16. High expectations — Your parents and teachers expect you to do your best at school and in other activities.

___ Yes ___ No

17. Creative activities — You participate in music, art, drama, or creative writing two or more times per week.

___ Yes ___ No

18. Child programs — You participate two or more times per week in co-curricular school activities or structured community programs for teens.

___ Yes ___ No

19. Religious community — You attend religious programs or services one or more times per week.

___ Yes ___ No

20. Time at home — You spend some time most days in high-quality interaction with parents and doing things at home other than watching TV or playing video games.

___ Yes ___ No

21. Achievement motivation — You are motivated and strive to do well in school.

___ Yes ___ No

22. Learning engagement — You are responsive, attentive, and actively engaged in learning at school and enjoy participating in learning activities outside of school.

___ Yes ___ No

Fair Use: Copies of this activity may be made for personal use. No mass production for distribution, or alteration of this activity is permitted without prior consent of the author.

23. **Homework** — You usually hand in homework on time.

    __ Yes __ No

24. **Bonding to school** — You care about teachers and other adults in your school.

    __ Yes __ No

25. **Reading for pleasure** — You enjoy reading for fun most days of the week.

    __ Yes __ No

26. **Caring** — Your parents tell you that it is important to help other people.

    __ Yes __ No

27. **Equality and social justice** — Your parents tell you that it is important to speak up for equal rights for all people.

    __ Yes __ No

28. **Integrity** — Your parents tell you that it is important to stand up for your beliefs.

    __ Yes __ No

29. **Honesty** — Your parents tell you that it is important to tell the truth.

    __ Yes __ No

30. **Responsibility** — Your parents tell you that it is important to accept personal responsibility for behavior.

    __ Yes __ No

31. **Healthy lifestyle** — Your parents tell you that it is important to make healthy decisions and have an understanding of healthy sexuality.

    __ Yes __ No

32. **Planning and decision making** — You think about decisions and are usually happy with results of your decisions.

    __ Yes __ No

33. **Interpersonal competence** — You care about and are affected by other people's feelings. You enjoy making friends and when frustrated or angry, try to calm yourself in healthy ways.

    __ Yes __ No

34. **Cultural competence** — You know and are comfortable with people of different racial, ethnic, and cultural backgrounds and have your own cultural identity.

    __ Yes __ No

Fair Use: Copies of this activity may be made for personal use. No mass production for distribution, or alteration of this activity is permitted without prior consent of the author.

35. **Resistance skills** — You can refuse people who are likely to get you in trouble. You are able to say no to things that are not healthy, legal and safe.

　 __ Yes __ No

36. **Conflict resolution skills** — You try to resolve conflicts non-violently.

　 __ Yes __ No

37. **Personal power** — You feel you have influence over things that happen in your life.

　 __ Yes __ No

38. **Self-esteem** — You like and are proud to be the person that you are.

　 __ Yes __ No

39. **Sense of purpose** — You sometimes think about what life means and whether there is a purpose for your life.

　 __ Yes __ No

40. **Positive view of personal future** — You are optimistic about your personal future.

　 __ Yes __ No

Copyright © 2003, 2006 by Search Institute, 615 First Avenue N.E., Suite 125, Minneapolis, MN 55413; 800-888-7828; www.search-institute.org. All Rights Reserved. These are registered trademarks of Search Institute: Search Institute®, Developmental Assets® and Healthy Communities • Healthy Youth®.

Pre-teen:

After assessing yourself on developmental assets, discuss with your parents/guardians their perception of the assets you possess. *Pay particular attention to those assets about which you and your parents have a different perception.* This discussion will definitely assist in building a trust between you and your parent that is critical in your life right now. When that discussion is complete, work on the Parent-Teen Asset Contract together!

Fair Use: Copies of this activity may be made for personal use. No mass production for distribution, or alteration of this activity is permitted without prior consent of the author.

PARENT

Asset Assessment Checklist

Check yes or no to each asset indicating whether YOU perceive your pre-teen has that asset or not.

1. **Family support** — Family life provides high levels of love and support.

    __ Yes __ No

2. **Positive family communication** — Parents and child communicate positively. Child feels comfortable seeking advice and counsel from parents.

    __ Yes __ No

3. **Other adult relationships** — Child receives support from adults other than her or his parents.

    __ Yes __ No

4. **Caring neighborhood** — Child experiences caring neighbors.

    __ Yes __ No

5. **Caring school climate** — Relationships with teachers and peers provide a caring, encouraging environment.

    __ Yes __ No

6. **Parent involvement in schooling** — Parents are actively involved in helping the child succeed in school.

    __ Yes __ No

7. **Community values youth** — Child feels valued and appreciated by adults in the community.

    __ Yes __ No

8. **Children as resources** — Child is included in decisions at home and in the community.

    __ Yes __ No

9. **Service to others** — Child has opportunities to help others in the community.

    __ Yes __ No

10. **Safety** — Child feels safe at home, at school, and in his or her neighborhood.

    __ Yes __ No

Fair Use: Copies of this activity may be made for personal use. No mass production for distribution, or alteration of this activity is permitted without prior consent of the author.

11. **Family boundaries** — Family has clear and consistent rules and consequences and monitors the child's whereabouts.

    __ Yes __ No

12. **School boundaries** — School provides clear rules and consequences.

    __ Yes __ No

13. **Neighborhood boundaries** — Neighbors take responsibility for monitoring the child's behavior.

    __ Yes __ No

14. **Adult role models** — Parents and other adults in the child's family, as well as nonfamily adults, model positive, responsible behavior.

    __ Yes __ No

15. **Friends** — Child's closest friends model positive, responsible behavior.

    __ Yes __ No

16. **High expectations** — Parents and teachers expect the child to do her or his best at school and in other activities.

    __ Yes __ No

17. **Creative activities**—Child participates in music, art, drama, or creative writing two or more times per week.

    __ Yes __ No

18. **Child programs** — Child participates two or more times per week in co-curricular school activities or structured community programs for children.

    __ Yes __ No

19. **Religious community** — Child attends religious programs or services one or more times per week.

    __ Yes __ No

20. **Time at home** — Child spends some time most days both in high-quality interaction with parents and doing things at home other than watching TV or playing video games.

    __ Yes __ No

21. **Achievement motivation** — Child is motivated and strives to do well in school.

    __ Yes __ No

22. **Learning engagement** — Child is responsive, attentive, and actively engaged in learning at school and enjoys participating in learning activities outside of school.

    __ Yes __ No

Fair Use: Copies of this activity may be made for personal use. No mass production for distribution, or alteration of this activity is permitted without prior consent of the author.

23. **Homework** — Child usually hands in homework on time.

    ___ Yes ___ No

24. **Bonding to school** — Child cares about teachers and other adults at school.

    ___ Yes ___ No

25. **Reading for pleasure** — Child enjoys and engages in reading for fun most days of the week.

    ___ Yes ___ No

26. **Caring** — Parents tell the child it is important to help other people.

    ___ Yes ___ No

27. **Equality and social justice** — Parents tell the child it is important to speak up for equal rights for all people.

    ___ Yes ___ No

28. **Integrity** — Parents tell the child it is important to stand up for one's beliefs.

    ___ Yes ___ No

29. **Honesty** — Parents tell the child it is important to tell the truth.

    ___ Yes ___ No

30. **Responsibility** — Parents tell the child it is important to accept personal responsibility for behavior.

    ___ Yes ___ No

31. **Healthy lifestyle** — Parents tell the child it is important to have good health habits and an understanding of healthy sexuality.

    ___ Yes ___ No

32. **Planning and decision making** — Child thinks about decisions and is usually happy with results of her or his decisions.

    ___ Yes ___ No

33. **Interpersonal competence** — Child cares about and is affected by other people's feelings, enjoys making friends, and, when frustrated or angry, tries to calm her or himself.

    ___ Yes ___ No

34. **Cultural competence** — Child knows and is comfortable with people of different racial, ethnic, and cultural backgrounds and with her or his own cultural identity.

    ___ Yes ___ No

Fair Use: Copies of this activity may be made for personal use. No mass production for distribution, or alteration of this activity is permitted without prior consent of the author.

35. **Resistance skills** — Child can stay away from people who are likely to get them in trouble. They are able to say no to things that are not healthy, legal and safe.

  __ Yes __ No

36. **Child seeks to resolve conflict nonviolently** — Child tries to resolve conflicts non-violently.

  __ Yes __ No

37. **Personal power** — Child feels he or she has some influence over things that happen in her or his life.

  __ Yes __ No

38. **Self-esteem** — Child likes and is proud to be the person that he or she is.

  __ Yes __ No

39. **Sense of purpose** — Child sometimes thinks about what life means and whether there is a purpose for her or his life.

  __ Yes __ No

40. **Positive view of personal future** — Child is optimistic about her or his personal future.

  __ Yes __ No

Copyright © 2003, 2006 by Search Institute, 615 First Avenue N.E., Suite 125, Minneapolis, MN 55413; 800-888-7828; www.search-institute.org. All Rights Reserved. These are registered trademarks of Search Institute: Search Institute®, Developmental Assets® and Healthy Communities • Healthy Youth®.

Parent:

After assessing your pre-teen's developmental assets, discuss with her or him their perception of the assets they possess. *Pay particular attention to those assets about which you and your child have a different perception.* This discussion will definitely assist in building a trust between you and your pre-teen that is critical to them in their life right now. When that discussion is complete, work on the Parent-Teen Asset Contract together!

Fair Use: Copies of this activity may be made for personal use. No mass production for distribution, or alteration of this activity is permitted without prior consent of the author.

Interactive Activity #2 Asset Contract

Parent and Pre-teen: After completing the checklist separately, compare the results each of you got. Discuss your thoughts and feelings, and **work together** on any 3 assets that either need to be attained OR maintained. Fill out the contract below to help you both do your part in the asset fulfillment. Use the S.M.A.R.T. principle to write out actions that will guide you in achieving your asset goals! Your actions need to be:

S=**S**pecific, **M**=**M**easurable, **A**=**A**ction-related, **R**=**R**ealistic, **T**=**T**ime-bound

Hard work on this contract can pay big dividends in future happiness and success! Take it seriously and work towards a GREAT LIFE!!!

Asset #1 _____

As parents we will:
_____
_____
_____

As a pre-teen I will:
_____
_____
_____

Fair Use: Copies of this activity may be made for personal use. No mass production for distribution, or alteration of this activity is permitted without prior consent of the author.

Asset #2_____

As parents we will:
_____
_____

As a pre-teen I will:
_____
_____
_____

Asset #3_____

As parents we will:
_____
_____

As a pre-teen I will:
_____
_____
_____

We, _____ (as parents), will agree to assist our pre-teen in attaining and maintaining all of the 40 assets but specifically the 3 assets listed above.

I, _____ (as pre-teen) will agree to work diligently to attain and maintain all 40 assets but specifically the 3 assets listed above.

_____   _____
Parent/guardian/mentor signature(s)   Date   Pre-teen signature   Date

Fair Use: Copies of this activity may be made for personal use. No mass production for distribution, or alteration of this activity is permitted without prior consent of the author.

Interactive Activity #3

Life Decisions with Impact!

Parent: With this activity you will have your pre-teen think about and then write the many consequences of specific decisions using an "impact wheel." Again, set a specific time and place for the two of you to brainstorm regarding a couple of the decisions from the list at a time. Ask your pre-teen to choose two decisions from the list at a time, and brainstorm ALL of the potential consequences that may stem from those decisions using the impact wheel worksheet.

Make as many copies of the impact wheel as you need; one for each decision that your child works through. After each is done, discuss the possible consequences they were able to imagine. Discuss why some teens continue to make unhealthy decisions despite these consequences. Understand that the portion of your pre-teen's brain that controls impulsivity and the ability to think of consequences doesn't develop until they are approximately 21 years of age.

You may need to assist your pre-teen in seeing consequences their lack of experience or immaturity prevents them from seeing on their own.

Pre-teen: Pick a couple of the decisions from the brainstorming page. Work on them, one at a time, using an impact wheel sheet. Write the name of the decision you have chosen in the center circle. Then write four possible consequences of that decision in the four attached circles. After that is done, identify three more specific consequences that could stem from each of those consequences. Write them in the three circles attached to each of the other consequences. When finished, you and your parent can discuss how one decision can cause sixteen or more unanticipated consequences. This exercise clearly illustrates the need to make the best decision possible in every situation. Good decisions create good consequences; bad decisions lead to bad consequences.

Parent and Pre-teen: Discuss how this exercise shows that pre-teens CAN identify many consequences of their choices IF they intentionally think about them ahead of time while not under the influence of alcohol, drugs and/or hormones! Also discuss not only what decisions your pre-teen intends to make but what plan they have to assure that they will make the best decision. Move to the next decision(s) until ALL are examined using the impact wheel.

Fair Use: Copies of this activity may be made for personal use. No mass production for distribution, or alteration of this activity is permitted without prior consent of the author.

An example: Acquiring a false ID.

Four consequences of that specific choice may be:

      1 – Get caught by police

      2 – Get into drinking establishments underage and become addicted at early age

      3 – Get the bar/tavern/dance club in trouble (fined) for serving an underage minor

      4 – Lose trust with your parents

Three consequences stemming from #1 might be: reputation tarnished, acquiring a police record, insurance RATES GO UP.

Three consequences stemming from #2 might be: trouble with law, may lose family, poor relationships.

Three consequences stemming from #3 might be: have to pay a fine, lose trust with adults, acquiring a police record.

Three consequences stemming from #4 might be: may lose the right to drive a car, may not be allowed to hang with present friends, may not be allowed to attend events, etc.

NOTE: All of those consequences also have consequences.

Fair Use: Copies of this activity may be made for personal use. No mass production for distribution, or alteration of this activity is permitted without prior consent of the author.

IMPACT DECISIONS FOR BRAINSTORMING

Brainstorm the consequences of these decisions one at a time:

- Alcohol use before the age of 21
- No alcohol use before the age of 21
- Smoking cigarettes
- Not smoking cigarettes
- Using drugs
- Not using drugs
- Riding with a driver who has been either drinking or is texting
- Choosing not to ride with a driver who has been drinking or who texts while driving
- Driving under the influence of alcohol, marijuana or other drugs
- Not driving under the influence of alcohol, marijuana or other drugs
- Being sexually active in a relationship
- Not being sexually active in a relationship
- Having sexual intercourse in a teen relationship
- Not having sexual intercourse in a teen relationship
- Bullying classmates
- Not bullying classmates

Fair Use: Copies of this activity may be made for personal use. No mass production for distribution, or alteration of this activity is permitted without prior consent of the author.

IMPACT WHEEL

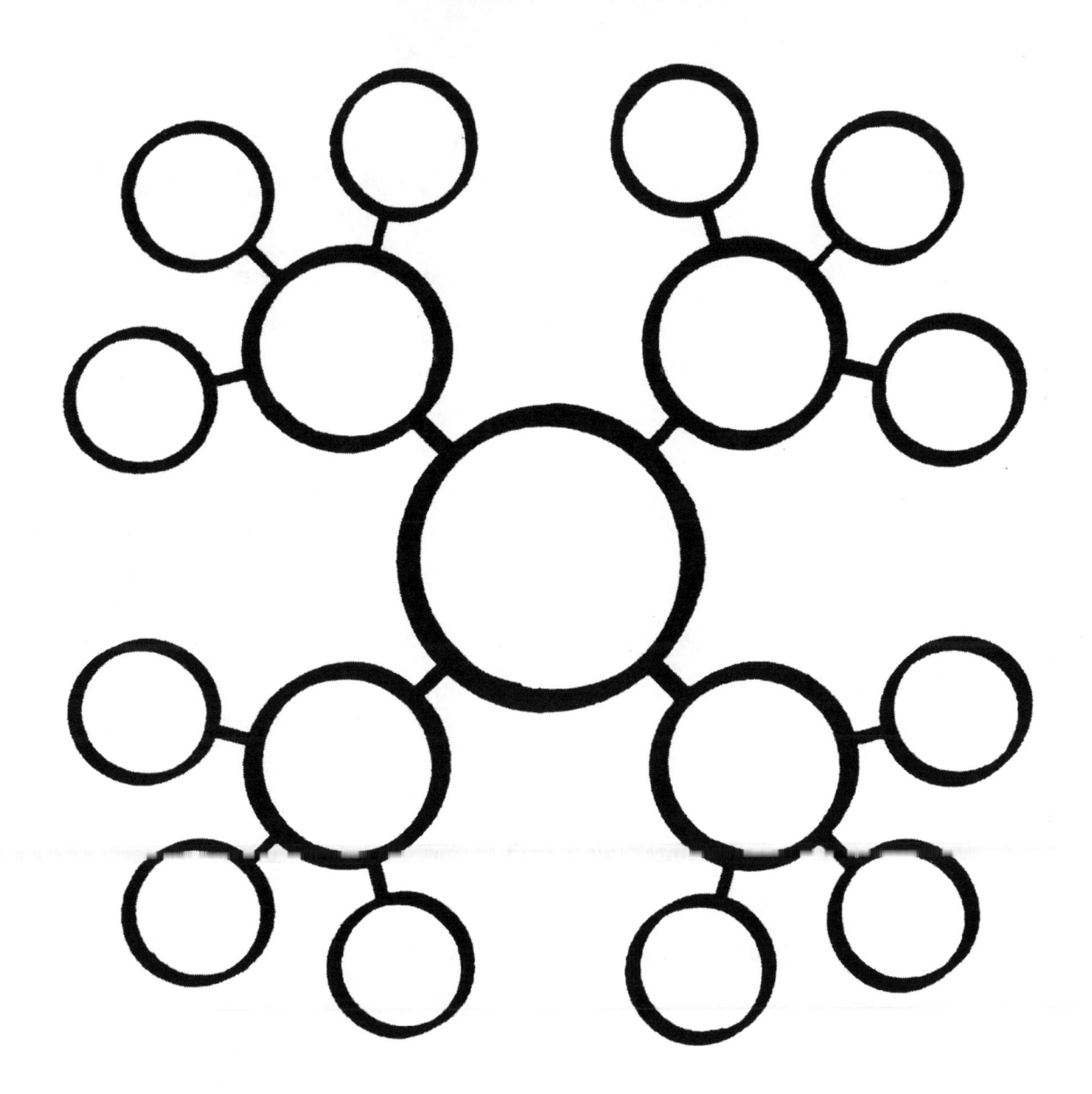

Activity #4

Goals, Wishes and Dreams….!

Parent: Begin by brainstorming the goals, wishes and dreams you have for your teen. Two interactive, brainstorming, identification and sharing activities are provided that will enable this to happen. Take some time with these activities. Teens with *written* goals and wishes accomplish many more of them than those that either don't have goals or don't write them down.

Teen: Begin by brainstorming and identifying your goals, wishes and dreams. Two interactive, brainstorming, identification and sharing activities are provided that will allow this to happen. Take some time with these activities and know that if you have *written* goals and wishes, you accomplish many more than teens that either don't have goals or don't write them down.

Parent and Pre-teen:

First activity: Parents identify the goals, wishes and dreams they have *for their teen* on the Parent Goals, Wishes and Dreams worksheet. The pre-teen identifies the goals, wishes and dreams she or he has on the Pre-teen Goals, Wishes and Dreams worksheet. After both are completed, discuss each other's list focusing on actions that need to occur over the next 10 years to allow these goals and wishes to be realized.

Second activity: Parents write a "Bucket List" – things they would like to do (or do again), experiences they'd like to have, places they'd like to go, etc. – before they die (or "kick the bucket"). This can be done on the worksheet called, "My Bucket List for Parents."

Fair Use: Copies of this activity may be made for personal use. No mass production for distribution, or alteration of this activity is permitted without prior consent of the author.

The pre-teen will also write out his or her own "Bucket List" – things they would like to do, experiences they'd like to have, places they'd like to go, etc. – before they die (or "kick the bucket"). This can be done on the worksheet called, **"My Bucket List for Pre-teens."**

After these are done and shared, both parties will write a Parent- Pre-teen Bucket List – things they would like to do together, experiences they'd like to have together, places they'd like to go together, etc. before they die. This can be done on the worksheet called, "Our Parent- Pre-teen Bucket List."

Creating and discussing Bucket Lists can be one of the most enjoyable activities you do together as parent and pre-teen. Be sure to talk about the way in which decisions a person makes day-to-day affect their ability to achieve their goals and wishes. Identify actions that need to be taken to assure that these goals and wishes will be realized. Remember, these are working documents and can be changed at any time! Don't forget to date and post them in a mutually visible site.

Fair Use: Copies of this activity may be made for personal use. No mass production for distribution, or alteration of this activity is permitted without prior consent of the author.

Goals, Wishes and Dreams
(Parents' Brainstorming Sheet)

Write the goals, wishes and dreams **YOU HAVE FOR YOUR PRE-TEEN!**

My goals, wishes and dreams for my pre-teen, 2-5 years from now (MS and HS) are:

1. _____

2. _____

3. _____

My goals, wishes and dreams for my pre-teen 6-10 years from now (Post HS/College) are:

1. _____

2. _____

3. _____

My goals, wishes and dreams for my pre-teen 11-15 years from now (Post College/Marriage/Parenting/Etc.) are:

1. _____

2. _____

3. _____

Decisions YOU think your pre-teen ought to consider to be able to secure these goals:

1. _____

2. _____

3. _____

Fair Use: Copies of this activity may be made for personal use. No mass production for distribution, or alteration of this activity is permitted without prior consent of the author.

Goals, Wishes and Dreams
(Pre-teen Brainstorming Sheet)

Write the goals, wishes and dreams **YOU HAVE FOR YOURSELF:**

My goals, wishes and dreams in 2-5 years from now (Middle School and High School) are:

1. _____
2. _____
3. _____

My goals, wishes and dreams in 6-10 years from now (Post High School/College) are:

1. _____
2. _____
3. _____

My goals, wishes and dreams in 11-15 years from now (Post College/Marriage/Parenting/Etc.) are:

1. _____
2. _____
3. _____

Goals can be achieved more effectively when you plan specific decisions/activities that will move you towards those desired goals. Continue thinking about this as you write your "Goal Achievement Plan" below.

Fair Use: Copies of this activity may be made for personal use. No mass production for distribution, or alteration of this activity is permitted without prior consent of the author.

Goal Achievement Plan

Pre-teen: Choose any goal from each section on your previous goal worksheet. Identify the specific decisions and activities you need to consider to help you achieve that goal. When done, discuss with your parents your goals, wishes and dreams and the specific plans you need to consider to acquire them.

Middle School/High School Goal: _____

_____

Decisions/Activities:

1. _____

2. _____

3. _____

Post High School/College Goal: _____

_____

Decisions/Activities:

1. _____

2. _____

3. _____

Job Acquisition/Marriage?/Parenting? Goal: _____

Decisions/Activities:

1. _____

2. _____

3. _____

Fair Use: Copies of this activity may be made for personal use. No mass production for distribution, or alteration of this activity is permitted without prior consent of the author.

Parent Bucket List

Parents: Create your bucket list in the space provided below. Again, these are things you would like to do (or do again) – experiences you'd like to have, places you'd like to go, etc. before you die (or "kick the bucket").

1. _____
2. _____
3. _____
4. _____
5. _____
6. _____
7. _____
8. _____
9. _____
10. _____
11. _____
12. _____
13. _____
14. _____
15. _____

Date:_____ Signature:_____

Fair Use: Copies of this activity may be made for personal use. No mass production for distribution, or alteration of this activity is permitted without prior consent of the author.

Teen Bucket List

Teen: Create your bucket list here. Again, these are things you would like to do (or do again) – experiences you'd like to have, places you'd like to go, etc. before you die (or "kick the bucket").

1. _____
2. _____
3. _____
4. _____
5. _____
6. _____
7. _____
8. _____
9. _____
10. _____
11. _____
12. _____
13. _____
14. _____
15. _____

Date:_____ Signature:_____

Fair Use: Copies of this activity may be made for personal use. No mass production for distribution, or alteration of this activity is permitted without prior consent of the author.

Parent-Pre-teen Bucket List

Parent-Pre-teen: Create a mutual bucket list here. Again, these are things you would like to do **together** (or do again **together**) – experiences both of you would like to have **together**, places you'd like to go **together**, etc. before you die (or "kick the bucket").

1. _____
2. _____
3. _____
4. _____
5. _____
6. _____
7. _____
8. _____
9. _____
10. _____
11. _____
12. _____
13. _____
14. _____
15. _____

Date:_____ Signatures:_____

Fair Use: Copies of this activity may be made for personal use. No mass production for distribution, or alteration of this activity is permitted without prior consent of the author.

Interactive Activity #5

Creating Healthy Teen Relationships...!

To determine what it takes to create healthy relationships, a discussion has to occur regarding the qualities that constitute a healthy relationship and the decisions one has to make that will allow it to develop. A good starting point is to look at good relationships you may presently be in and identify those characteristics you feel are making the relationship a healthy one. Utilize the following interactive discussion worksheet to strategize together to develop strong, healthy relationships.

Discuss as parent and pre-teen:

- What makes your present friendships and/or other relationships healthy?

- What kinds of relationships are healthy and appropriate for pre-teens in middle school? For teens in high school?

- What kinds of relationships are healthy and appropriate for college-aged students?

- What are some reasons to have several relationships as you develop through your teen years?

- Why is it important to ask others how they view your relationship(s)?

- How would alcohol use, drug use and or sexual activity reduce the chances for a healthy relationship to occur?

- What kinds of relationships do you want as a pre-teen?

- What decisions do you need to make now in order for those healthy relationships to happen?

- What are the important aspects of communication in a healthy relationship?

Fair Use: Copies of this activity may be made for personal use. No mass production for distribution, or alteration of this activity is permitted without prior consent of the author.

Fair Use: Copies of this activity may be made for personal use. No mass production for distribution, or alteration of this activity is permitted without prior consent of the author.

Interactive Activity #6

Consequences, Consequences, Consequences…
Pre- and Teen-age Sexual Relationships!

Parent:

Clarify with your pre-teen the terms "sex," "sexual activity" and "sexual intercourse."

Discuss "typical questions pre-teens have about sex."

- When I feel pressured to engage in sexual activity, how do I say no without making my boyfriend or girlfriend feel bad?

- How far is too far when it comes to "sexual activity?"

- Why do many teens have sexual intercourse before marriage?

- When is it okay to have sexual intercourse?

- Can you get pregnant the first time you have sexual intercourse?

- What is a condom? What is a female condom?

- Can you get pregnant while having your period?

Fair Use: Copies of this activity may be made for personal use. No mass production for distribution, or alteration of this activity is permitted without prior consent of the author.

THE CONSEQUENCES:

Ask your pre-teen the following question:

"What do you think most teens worry about after they have had sexual intercourse for the first time?"

Discuss the consequences, listed below, *other than pregnancy*, of early sexual activity in teen relationships. Point out that these consequences were drawn from interviews with teens who had been sexually active or had engaged in sexual intercourse.

After discussing the consequences listed below, use the questions at the end of the worksheet as the basis of a meaningful conversation with your pre-teen.

Basically the same mental, emotional, social, financial and physical consequences are endured by girls and guys alike, BUT BOYS DON'T GET PREGNANT! So, quite often guys tend to take more risks when it comes to being sexually active. Girls need to know this.

As I travel the country, more and more young men are choosing abstinence and they are very proud of their decision.

Mental/Emotional Consequences of Early Sexual Activity:

- **Feel used/abused**
- **Feel guilty**
- **Feel confused**
- **Feel "empty"**
- **Feel afraid/scared**
- **Feel anxious/worried/nervous**
- **Feel depressed**
- **Develop a lower self-esteem**
- **Begin to lose self-confidence**
- **Begin to think that other unhealthy behaviors are okay**

Fair Use: Copies of this activity may be made for personal use. No mass production for distribution, or alteration of this activity is permitted without prior consent of the author.

Social Consequences of Early Sexual Activity:

- Loss of close friends who aren't sexually active
- Reputation is tarnished
- Future relationships may be affected
- Loss of trust with parents
- Increase in popularity with sexually-active peers
- Decrease in popularity with non-sexually-active peers

Financial Consequences of Early Sexual Activity:

- Possible pregnancy testing
- S.T.I. testing
- Doctor check-ups
- Contraception costs
- Abortion costs
- Birthing costs
- Alimony/child support for 18 years (It has been estimated that it costs approximately $245,360 to raise a child to age 18 in today's economy!)

Physical Consequences of Early Sexual Activity: (I share this category last since most teens think of these first!)

- May get a sexually transmitted infection (S.T.I.)
- May develop cervical cancer from acquiring the S.T. I. – HPV (human papilloma virus)
- May have to have a hysterectomy (removal of uterus) then be unable to have children in the future.
- May get AIDS
- May get physically addicted to alcohol/drugs and have to deal with the mental consequences
- **Last of all,** I (my girlfriend) may get pregnant and develop stretch marks on my/her body.

Fair Use: Copies of this activity may be made for personal use. No mass production for distribution, or alteration of this activity is permitted without prior consent of the author.

Parent-pre-teen discussions questions:

- Why do teens who have had sexual intercourse immediately only worry about pregnancy as a consequence?

- Why do teens who become sexually active often feel trapped in that relationship?

- What challenges might there be in store for you as a pre-teen as you develop teen relationships?

- Thinking of the consequences you have been discussing, identify 10 reasons to not engage in sexual intercourse while in a teen relationship:

    1._____

    2._____

    3._____

    4._____

    5._____

    6._____

    7._____

    8._____

    9._____

    10._____

Fair Use: Copies of this activity may be made for personal use. No mass production for distribution, or alteration of this activity is permitted without prior consent of the author.

Interactive Activity #7

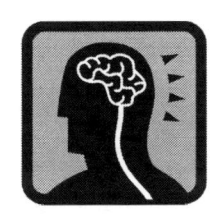

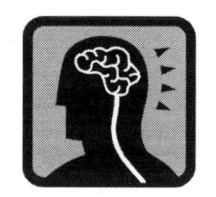

Hormones Out of Control....!

There are several situations where the chances of reaching the "danger zone" are quite high.

Parents: Begin this interactive activity with your pre-teen by reviewing the continuum that describes "sexual activity" in a teen relationship:

		<<<DANGER ZONE>>>	
Stage 1	Stage 2	Stage 3	Stage 4
Attraction	Dating / "Going Out"	Physical Intimacy	Sexual Intercourse

Stage 1:

Most pre-teen relationships start pretty simply. Back "in the day" pre-teens often started the process by passing notes to someone they liked. You remember them: check the box if you like me, and check the box if you want to "go out." It makes us smile to look back on those behaviors. In that attraction stage a smile from someone you admired could make you feel warm all over! Another early pre-teen ritual was "sending in the troops;" sending all of your friends to the one you liked to ask if they like you! Are the memories coming back? This stage also included talking on the phone, (today it would be "texting") and maybe hanging out in safe groups of mixed gender kids, but always trying to be in the same group with that person you felt was special. Few problems with that stage in a relationship, back then or today.

Stage 2:

When teens begin dating, they assume that they are "going out" or "going together" and there is usually an understanding that they should be true to each other and not date anyone else. In many cases today, that has changed with the social freedom of having "friends with benefits." "Friends with benefits" describes a temporary and sometimes serial relationship in which it is understood that sexual "benefits" will be granted during the "date" with no long-term expectations or obligations. Needless to say, these are unhealthy and dangerous relationships. Most teens in this second stage hold hands, kiss and hug each other, go out to movies and athletic events, buy each other gifts and just hang out watching TV. Responsible teens in a healthy relationship are able to behave appropriately in this stage when they are alone but are also comfortable when they are in social situations with adults. Mature young people who understand and adhere to the continuum can thrive here and have an enjoyable and healthy relationship.

Fair Use: Copies of this activity may be made for personal use. No mass production for distribution, or alteration of this activity is permitted without prior consent of the author.

Stage 3—beginning of the "danger zone:"

I call this stage the "physical intimacy stage." Here's where we lose many of our teens to the power of hormones! If sexual advances are made by one or both parties in a relationship they can elicit dangerous hormonal explosions. I truly believe that being under the influence of hormones can be just as dangerous as being under the influence of alcohol and or drugs. And yes, many teens are often under the influence of both, making it a double-whammy.

It is in this stage that the danger zone begins. Teens may "French kiss" in lieu of a normal appropriate friendship kiss. They may "pet," "paw," or caress each other in areas of privacy. They may fondle each other. Some teens acquire hickeys in this stage. Others "practice" oral sex and believe that it is much safer than sexual intercourse. What they don't understand is that they can acquire S.T.I.s in their mouths and down their throats. And, for three of the many S.T.I.s pre-teens can contract, we simply don't have a cure! Once acquired, they have them for life! Others quite often experiment with various other inappropriate sexual activities where "the sky is the limit." During this stage hormones take over their bodies making them feel very good. Emotions begin to guide their mind and their bodies. Common sense is greatly diminished. Thinking of any consequences is rendered virtually impossible.

Stage 4:

Most teens enter stage four drunk, high on drugs or heavily under the influence of hormones and end up "going all the way" and having sexual intercourse. In most cases, once they have experienced sexual intercourse they will continue to engage in it, especially if there were no major consequences the first few times. Teen pregnancies, S.T.I.s and many other unwanted consequences await them.

Parents/Pre-teens: After reviewing and discussing this continuum together, it's time to talk about specific situations that increase the chances of entering the danger zone and beginning a sexually active teen relationship. Here are some situations that have been shared with me by teens from all over the country.

- Under the influence of alcohol
- Under the influence of a drug(s)
- Long periods of time alone
- Periods of time alone in dark areas
- Periods of time with no adult supervision
- Casual and occasional kissing morphs into regular and passionate kissing
- Casual and occasional hugging morphs into regular and passionate hugging
- Casual and occasional touching morphs into regular and passionate touching
- A casual and occasional message morphs into a regular and passionate message

Fair Use: Copies of this activity may be made for personal use. No mass production for distribution, or alteration of this activity is permitted without prior consent of the author.

- After or while watching sexually explicit TV shows/unsupervised sexually rated movies/porn sites
- After talking about or texting sexually explicit messages or pictures (sexting)
- After or while listening to sexually explicit music
- After snuggling or lying near each other on a couch, sofa, beach, etc.
- After troubled arguments with parents or friends when you feel your mental, emotional and maybe even your physical needs haven't been met
- Attending parties where "friends with benefits" is the accepted rule
- Combinations of several of these – increasing the power immensely!

Parents: Ask your pre-teen what they *could do* and what they *could say* to prevent these situations which may lead them into the "danger zone."

Fair Use: Copies of this activity may be made for personal use. No mass production for distribution, or alteration of this activity is permitted without prior consent of the author.

Interactive Activity #8

Pros and Cons of Abstinence!

Parents: In this activity with your pre-teen, you will discuss the term abstinence. Abstinence, as you will be defining it in your discussion, applies to more than just sexual intercourse. You and your pre-teen will look objectively at, and discuss, the "pros" and "cons" of postponing sexual activity in teen relationships. The "pros" then need to be focused on because they act as motivators for delaying sexual intercourse. The pre-teen will identify, from this worksheet, their own valid reasons to delay sexual activity. Those reasons can then can be used as the basis of a parent-pre-teen contract signed by parties.

NOTE:

- Although I have listed several consequences of abstinence, my intention is to have you and your pre-teen spend most of your discussion time focusing on the benefits of abstinence.
- Discuss the pros and cons from the viewpoint of all mental, emotional, social, financial as well as physical consequences.
-

"CONS"	"PROS"
May not be asked out	i.e. Don't have to worry about a pregnancy
May not be able to go out with the person you like	_____
May spend some lonely nights	_____
May get ridiculed or pressured	_____
May not date until you are older	_____
May lose a person you like to someone else	_____
May feel immature	_____
Texting with friends may diminish	_____
Could be tempted to go on porn sites	_____
Could be tempted to look for "sex" in porn magazines, etc.	_____

Fair Use: Copies of this activity may be made for personal use. No mass production for distribution, or alteration of this activity is permitted without prior consent of the author.

Parent-teen Abstinence Contract

My valid reasons to delay sexual activity:

1. _____

2. _____

3. _____

4. _____

5. _____

6. _____

7. _____

8. _____

9. _____

10. _____

_____

Teen Signature   Date

_____   _____

Parent Signature   Date   Parent Signature   Date

Fair Use: Copies of this activity may be made for personal use. No mass production for distribution, or alteration of this activity is permitted without prior consent of the author.

Interactive Activity #9

Life Skills: My Toolbox for Life!

Parents: It is now time for you to discuss, teach and practice the following life skills with your pre-teen:

- Assertiveness skill
- Quick and healthy decision-making skill
- Problem-solving skill
- Communication skill
- Active-listening skill
- "Know" skill
- Care-frontation skill

After discussing these skills with your pre-teen, practice the skills using scenarios involving alcohol, drugs and sexual activities. One example of a scenario is given for each skill. You and your pre-teen can create realistic scenarios for the other situations. Use them as "tools" for your life!

PRACTICE-PRACTICE-PRACTICE = EMPOWERED TEEN!

Assertiveness skill:

This life skill allows a teen to effectively stand up for what they believe is healthy, legal and safe and state their position in a calm, caring, respectful manner while remaining in control.

- **Alcohol scenario:** (User created scenario)

- **Drugs scenario:**

    You are at a party with a lot of your classmates and friends. Without notice, someone hands a "pass around" joint to you. How would you act assertively? What would you say?

- **Sexual pressure scenario**: (User created scenario)

Fair Use: Copies of this activity may be made for personal use. No mass production for distribution, or alteration of this activity is permitted without prior consent of the author.

Quick and healthy decision-making skill:

This is an powerful life skill that will allow your pre-teen to quickly decide when faced with a dangerous, illegal or unhealthy choice. It has to be used without being under the influence of alcohol, drugs or hormones. It simply won't be remembered or utilized in those three situations. It is used when your pre-teen doesn't have a lot of time to make their decision. This skill, when learned and practiced, can be effectively utilized in 10-15 seconds! When your teen is faced with a decision they simply ask themselves five quick questions within 10-15 seconds. These questions include:

- **Is it healthy?**
- **Is it safe?**
- **Is it legal?**
- **Does it respect the wishes of my parents?**
- **Does it respect my wishes and wishes of others?**

IF the answer to any of these questions is NO they should be assertive and decide not do it. IF they decide to go ahead, they had better be ready for ANY of the consequences that could occur. Pre-teens can learn this skill fairly easily and, if utilized on a regular basis, it can save them having to deal with many unnecessary consequences throughout their developmental years. You will easily see many of these life skills are dependent on each other. For instance, after using the quick and healthy decision-making skill, they'll need to be assertive when stating their decision.

- **Alcohol scenario:** (User created scenario)
- **Drugs scenario:** (User created scenario)
- **Sexual pressure scenario:**

    You've been "going out" with this person for eight months. You really like them a lot. You have not been sexually active at all but lately have felt a bit of pressure from your partner. You are talking with them after school near your locker. They have invited you over to their house tonight and have stated, "My parents won't be home and we'll have the whole house to ourselves." Use the decision-making skill to decide whether or not you should accept their offer.

Fair Use: Copies of this activity may be made for personal use. No mass production for distribution, or alteration of this activity is permitted without prior consent of the author.

Problem-solving skill:

We all need help solving issues and problems that crop up in our lives. Pre-teens especially need to be taught this basic life skill to allow them to work through their own issues when adult help isn't available or when they don't necessarily want anyone else's input. Most teens do not know how to solve problems due to their lack of life experience so we need to teach them. This skill is directly involved with making your pre-teen an independent thinker and problem-solver.

The steps in this skill include:

- **Identify the specific issue or problem**
- **Brainstorm and write down a list of all possible ways of dealing with the issue**
- **List the "pros" and "cons" of each possible choice**
- **Choose one choice**
- **Use the quick and healthy decision-making skill to help you decide**
- **Make a decision**
- **Evaluate**

- **Alcohol scenario:**

    You are invited to a party Friday night where many of your classmates will be. There is a person that you really like that is also planning to attend. You do understand that alcohol will be served. The person you like asks you to attend and "hang out." You are out for athletics and don't drink alcohol. You want to go to be with your friend but you don't want to drink or be at a party with underage drinking. YOU HAVE A PROBLEM! Use the problem-solving skill to help you resolve the problem!

- **Drugs scenario:** (User created scenario)
- **Sexual pressure scenario:** (User created scenario)

Fair Use: Copies of this activity may be made for personal use. No mass production for distribution, or alteration of this activity is permitted without prior consent of the author.

Communication skill:

This life skill can be utilized by both parents and pre-teens to enhance communication immediately. It is non-judgmental, non-accusatory and allows both parties to express their feelings and say what they want or need. Parents can become proficient in this skill and begin practicing it in their day-to-day communication with each other. It is often called the "I" formula because it starts with an "I" statement.

Here are the specific steps of the communication life skill:

- **Say the person's name** you intend to communicate with to secure their attention
- Say …. **"I feel"**….
  Here, one shares an emotion they are feeling. Feelings might include anger, frustration, confusion, worry, etc.
- Next say …. **"when"**…
  After the word "when," tell what the circumstance is that's causing your feeling. For example: "when I try and keep our home clean and things are thrown everywhere…."
- Then say …. **"because"**…
  After the word "because," tell how you are affected. For instance, "I have to spend a lot of my busy time picking up after everyone…"
- Continue with either:
  "What I want"…, **"What I would like"**…, or **"Would you consider?"**…
  In this step, specifically say what you want, need or would like them to consider!
- Finally, say **"Thank you"** or just **"thanks."**
  Complete the skill by simply thanking them ahead of time.

- **Alcohol scenario:**
  Your "date" is requesting you attend a party. You suspect there will be alcohol use and some drug use there. You really like your date a lot and are worried about attending the party and what your date will think of you if you don't attend. Use the communication skill to talk to your date. Say it out loud. Practice saying it to your parent.

- **Drugs scenario:** (User created scenario)
- **Sexual pressure scenario:** (User created scenario)

Fair Use: Copies of this activity may be made for personal use. No mass production for distribution, or alteration of this activity is permitted without prior consent of the author.

Active-listening skill:

This life skill takes practice because most of us don't listen very well. Parents need to pay attention to what their child is saying or feeling. When your pre-teen feels *heard*, they are more likely to compromise and resolve the conflict.

These 3 elements are crucial elements of active listening:

- **Paraphrasing:** periodically restating what was just said, putting it into your own words. You can do this by stating, "so what you're saying is….."
- **Validating:** questioning what you heard in order to be sure that what you are hearing is correct. You can do this by stating, "Did I hear you right when you said…."
- **Clarifying:** restating a word, phrase or concept when you were unclear about what you heard. You can do this by stating, "Did you just say, next year?"

Below are 5 guidelines to aid in your active listening:

- **Give encouragement** by raising eyebrows, looking your partner in their eyes and tilting your head slightly to show your willingness to truly listen. Try not to argue, blame moralize, judge, accuse, insult or threaten. Above all, DON'T INTERRUPT, AND DON'T JUMP IN AND COMPLETE THEIR SENTENCES!
- **Stay focused** on what the other person is saying and the feelings they are sharing.
- **Paraphrase, validate and clarify** when possible. Try not to be thinking of a response as you are listening.
- **Make verbal statements or non-verbal gestures** that suggest acceptance, understanding and appreciation.
- **Allow for some silence before you speak.** Allow yourself to assimilate what you heard.

Again, listening is hard work. It is a life skill that even adults need to practice and refine. Work on it with your spouse and or significant other. Then use it with you pre-teen.

Alcohol scenario: (User created scenario)

Drugs scenario: Your girlfriend/boyfriend/parent says, "you're really not listening to me when I talk to you." Practice apologizing, using the active listening skills you've learned.

Sexual pressure scenario: (User created scenario)

KNOW skill:

This is a powerful life skill not known, and thus not used, by many teenagers. It is not as simple as just saying "no." I believe our pre-teens and teens do need to know how to say, "No." But more, they need to know and utilize a specific life skill called the "KNOW" skill.

The skill has 2 goals:

- **To allow youth to say no and *still* keep their friends**
- **To allow youth to say no and *still* have fun**

Most pre-teens and teens today that I speak with say they would say "no" more often if they could say no and still have fun, keep their friends, stay out of trouble and be in control. Many youth say "yes" because they don't want to lose their friends and they want to have fun, two very important things in the life of a young person between the ages of 11-14.

Here are the 4 steps to the "KNOW" life skill:

- **Think about your decision.**
- **State *only one* consequence and repeat it.**
- **Offer and sell something else to do.**
- **Physically move as you invite your friends to "go along" with your suggestion.**

Think about your decision:

Step one: lets you quickly make a healthy, legal and safe decision. Your child should already know this skill. Remember, it is the one where they are to ask themselves the five questions to see if it is healthy, legal, safe, and in accord with their personal wishes and those of their parents? Also remember that this should only take 5-10 seconds. Let your child know that if they answer no to any one of the five questions, they should not do the thing they are being asked to do. If they make a decision that may be risky and unhealthy, they need to be ready for any of the consequences that may follow that decision. Speaking of consequences, if they still want to keep their friend, stay in control, stay out of trouble and still have fun, they need to proceed to the next step.

Step two: state *only one* consequence and repeat it. When your pre-teen is being pressured to do something they know they should not do they do not need to yield to the pressures put upon them. They need to assertively state *one* realistic, negative consequence. If pressure continues from their friend or peer, they need only to state *the same consequence* again. This is important as each time they state the same consequence, their friend or peer quickly realizes that the person they are pressuring has solidly made up their mind. Teach your teen to respond in a matter of fact tone and a confident manner. After the consequence has been stated a few times, your pre-teen needs to move to the next step.

Fair Use: Copies of this activity may be made for personal use. No mass production for distribution, or alteration of this activity is permitted without prior consent of the author.

Step three: persuade your friends to do something else. If friends keep the pressure on after hearing your pre-teen state his or her objection, giving the consequence that he or she is unwilling to risk, then it is time to suggest and sell an alternative that is at least equally or more inviting than his or her friends' proposal. If your child has no viable alternative to offer, they need to skip this step and go right to the final step. But, if they still want to have fun, keep their friends, and stay out of trouble, they need to offer an appealing alternative for their friends to consider. This is an invitation, if you will, to do something different that is healthy, legal and safe. If the friends still don't want to buy into the alternative suggestion, it is imperative that your pre-teen immediately goes to the final step.

Step four: physically move away as you invite you friends to join you in *your* decision. This is the most powerful step and allows teens to refuse effectively. Most teens sit and debate the alternatives until they get broken down. Here, your pre-teen actually starts to walk away (if they can in the situation) and invites their friends to join him or her in making a better decision. The power is with your pre-teen here as the others pressuring her or him are forced to make a decision one way or another.

This skill, when used effectively, can give your child a very unique opportunity to "say no" and still keep their friends and have fun.

Alcohol scenario: (User created scenario)

Drugs scenario: (User created scenario)

Sexual pressure scenario: The person you have been going out with is talking to you at your locker during the lunch break at school. Out of the clear blue sky, they ask you, "Do you want to go out to my car during 6th period?" Use the refusal skill to ask questions. Before agreeing to their request, you find out they want to cuddle, kiss and get physically intimate while in the car. Use steps 2-5 in the refusal skill to refuse effectively stay out of trouble and still keep the relationship with a person you like.

PRACTICE—PRACTICE—PRACTICE
THESE LIFE SKILLS WILL EMPOWER YOU TO ENJOY MANY HEALTHY RELATIONSHIPS!

Fair Use: Copies of this activity may be made for personal use. No mass production for distribution, or alteration of this activity is permitted without prior consent of the author.

Care-frontation skill:

This skill is useful to both parents and their teens. It allows anyone concerned about another person's behavior to "confront" them in a very caring, non-threatening and non-judgmental manner.

The steps for the care-frontation life skill:

- Say their name
- Say, "I care/love/am concerned…"
- Say, "I see…"
- Say, "I feel…"
- Listen…..
- Say, "I want…"
- Say, "I will…"

Say their name:

To begin using this powerful skill, one has to say the name of the person they are confronting and are concerned about. This should be done assertively and in a low, caring, non-aggressive tone of voice.

Say "I care/love/am concerned…"

This step is a very important one. It allows the person who is concerned to state *why* they want to communicate with the other person. Depending on the relationship, the user of the skill states whether they care about, or love the person they are confronting. Something as simple as, "You've been a great friend of mine for a long time and I really do care a lot about you," often deflates any negative feelings that are usually present in a "confrontation." A short delay or brief time of silence after this statement can be very powerful.

Say, "I see…"

Here, you tell all the personally observed behaviors and known hard facts that you are concerned about. Notice I mentioned, personally observed behaviors and hard facts. Share *only* behaviors, concerns and facts that they cannot begin to deny or start to argue with. You don't want to get into what you've heard, or what others may think, which opens the door for them to begin negating those happenings. When communicating with them regarding what you have seen, share as many personally observable behaviors and known hard facts as you can.

Fair Use: Copies of this activity may be made for personal use. No mass production for distribution, or alteration of this activity is permitted without prior consent of the author.

Say, "I feel…"

Next, share an emotion or emotions you are feeling. A feeling is an emotion. Tune into what you are truly feeling and share it honestly. When done, open the door for communication by simply remaining quiet and not talking. Remember, silence is golden. Most people are moved by silence when they are confronted in a caring way.

Listen…

This actually is the hardest step. Allow for silence. Usually people check into their feelings and are thinking during this time! Most people want to immediately offer advice here – refrain. Allow the door to open so they begin to share.

Say, "I want…"

When you are done listening to them, state what you want and then move quickly to the last step.

Say, "I will…"

Tell them explicitly what you are willing to do to help them. Be specific and always follow through. This is what separates a normal confrontation with this "care-frontation" life skill.

Use this skill in your personal relationships before you teach it to your pre-teen. Find out how powerful it is! It is most effectively done face-to-face, less effective on the phone. But it can sometimes be partially successful by writing your concerns in a card or letter or by texting.

Alcohol scenario: You are very concerned that your friend's drinking is excessive and becoming a problem. You see her or him skipping school frequently, dropping out of previously important activities and letting his or her grades decline. You *care* about your friend a lot so you are very concerned. Use the care-frontation skill to confront and communicate your concern.

Drugs scenario: (User created scenario)

Sexual pressure scenario: (User created scenario)

By using these life skills "tools" you can build the framework of a healthy, happy and successful life for your pre-teen!

Fair Use: Copies of this activity may be made for personal use. No mass production for distribution, or alteration of this activity is permitted without prior consent of the author.

Interactive Activity #10

Am I Ready……?

Parents: After interactively working on activities 1-9 with your pre-teen, you need to give him or her an opportunity to see if he or she is ready for a healthy relationship. As the caring parent, ask your pre-teen the following questions. Stress to your child that it is important that they give you their most honest answers.

1. Do you understand most, if not all, the "Definition Missing" terms we discussed in activity one? (If they are unsure, try a few of the terms and see if they do know!)
2. Can you identify at least five developmental assets you need to focus on acquiring? What are they? If unsure, refer back to the assessments you took and discuss them once again.
3. Are you able to identify four immediate consequences of a behavior and then identify at least three consequences from those immediate ones? If you are unsure, try to name the consequences of underage drinking.
4. Will your goals, wishes and dreams guide your upcoming decisions? If so, name at least five of your goals, wishes, and dreams and state how a pregnancy could affect them.
5. Can you identify the important qualities that you would like to see in a healthy relationship that you may be in?
6. Are you aware of the many mental, emotional, social, financial and physical consequences of sexual intercourse in a teen relationship? If so, name two from each category.
7. Tell what you need to do and or what you need to say in situations that could lead you into the "danger zone" where hormones begin to control your thinking.
8. Do you have several valid reasons to postpone sexual activity and remain abstinent? Name them.
9. Can you effectively use all of the life skills you have learned with your parent in relevant situations in your life? If so, share what you know about three of them and how you might use those three in sexual pressure situations.
10. Are you aware of the responsible behaviors you need to display in order to establish a trusting relationship with your parent as you move into your teen years? Name at least five responsibilities.

Fair Use: Copies of this activity may be made for personal use. No mass production for distribution, or alteration of this activity is permitted without prior consent of the author.

Questions to ask your pre-teen or teen:

Unfortunately, many teens are involved in relationships that are hurtful. Most high school and college students know someone who has been beaten or hit by their partner.

Answer these question about your relationship

- Does your boyfriend or girlfriend respect you?
- Do you genuinely care about each other?
- Do you communicate openly?
- Do you trust each other?
- Do you share in decision making?
- Do you compromise when there is a disagreement?
- Do you take responsibility for each other's actions?

In most problem relationships one person wants to be in control. They want all your attention and want to spend all of their time with you. At first, this may seem flattering, but after a while it becomes suffocating or even scary.

Some warning signs are:

- Jealousy: accusing you of things you didn't do
- Making all of your decisions
- Not letting you hang out with your friends
- Telling you what to wear or how to act
- Texting or checking up on you all of the time
- Blaming you for problems: putting a guilt trip on you
- Hitting or hurting you
- Threatening you if you leave
- Forcing sex on you and refusing to practice "safer" sex

Being in a situation like the one described above might make you feel afraid, sad, angry, confused and even depressed. You may feel very lonely and too helpless or ashamed to tell anyone.

Fair Use: Copies of this activity may be made for personal use. No mass production for distribution, or alteration of this activity is permitted without prior consent of the author.

So how do you get out?

- **Tell a parent, mentor, friend or relative what is going on.**
- **Break up in a public place with a friend to support you.**
- **Change your route to school if need be.**
- **Use a "buddy system" when going out afterwards.**
- **Change e-mail/cell phone number/passwords if you have to.**
- **Find safe places to go – not house parties without adult supervision.**
- **Keep a journal/personal record of what happens afterwards and call police if you need to.**
- **Respect yourself and know that you deserve a healthy relationship.**
- **Call the National Dating Abuse Helpline for a live chat with adult counselors. 1-866-331-9474**

Fair Use: Copies of this activity may be made for personal use. No mass production for distribution, or alteration of this activity is permitted without prior consent of the author.

AM I READY.....?

Pre-teen: After answering all of the questions with your parents, and thinking about the things they just shared with you about what makes a good (or a troubled) relationship, complete the following exercise.

Write a handwritten letter to your parents giving several reasons why you think you are ready (or perhaps are NOT ready) to embark on a teen relationship. Text a letter to your parent if that is more comfortable for you.

Dear_____,
         Parent

_____
_____
_____
_____
_____
_____
_____
_____
_____
_____
_____
_____
_____
_____
_____
_____
_____
_____
_____
_____
_____

Pre-teen signature   Date

Fair Use: Copies of this activity may be made for personal use. No mass production for distribution, or alteration of this activity is permitted without prior consent of the author.

Interactive Activity #11

Mutual Expectations

It is clear that setting specific and attainable expectations for your teens are important. I am a firm believer in "contractual agreements." They establish higher accountability standards and provide a reason for imposing consequences should that need to be done. Having your teen sign a mutually agreed upon contract is crucial to their healthy decision-making and relationship development.

Parent:

Here, you will find an example of an Expectation Contract. It has several topics that you and your teen may want to discuss and then mutually agree on with reasonable expectations and their consequences if not met. There is also a blank permanent contract for you to fill out and each sign when your discussion on expectations concludes.

It is my hope that both the parent and pre-teen have gained valuable knowledge and skills working together in this interactive workbook. Your pre-teen can use their newly-gained knowledge, life skills and assets as he or she works on this expectations contract. Enjoy this trust-building and accountability exercise.

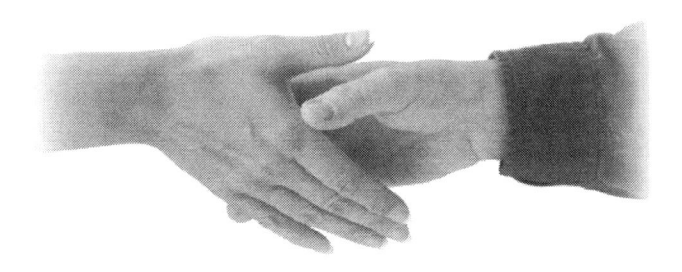

Fair Use: Copies of this activity may be made for personal use. No mass production for distribution, or alteration of this activity is permitted without prior consent of the author.

Mutual Expectations – (Example)

Discuss each topic in the left hand column, then agree on an expectation related to that topic. Finally, assign a mutually agreed upon consequence for failure to meet the expectation.

Topic	Expectation	Consequence if not met
Curfew	10:00 P.M. weekdays – 11:30 PM weekends	Lose trust / 1 weekend night at home
Riding with someone who has been drinking	Call parent for a ride at any time	Lose trust / No car for 1 week
Drinking and driving	Call parent for a ride at any time	Lose trust / pay fine / No car for six months
Texting and driving	Will not touch phone while driving – will use Bluetooth capabilities	Lose trust / pay ticket
Getting a speeding ticket	Drive the speed limit	Teen pays ticket and any increase in insurance cost
Alcohol use	No alcohol use	Lose trust / pay ticket
Drug use	No drug use	Lose trust / pay ticket / get drug and alcohol assessment
Setting sexual limits	No heavy petting or sexual intercourse	Lose trust / contract S.T.I.s / damage reputation
Danger Zone	Avoid high risk situations	Lose trust / pregnancy / damage career goals / trapped in relationship
Communication	Talk anytime	Grow apart / lose trust
Asset building	List deficiencies and work together on them	Fewer assets = more unhealthy behaviors More assets = greater success in life

_____   _____   _____
Date   Parents signatures   Teen signature

Fair Use: Copies of this activity may be made for personal use. No mass production for distribution, or alteration of this activity is permitted without prior consent of the author.

Mutual Expectations

Discuss each topic in the left hand column, then agree on an expectation related to that topic. Finally, assign a mutually agreed upon consequence for failure to meet the expectation.

Topic	**Expectation**	**Consequence if not met**
Curfew	_____	_____
Riding with someone who has been drinking	_____	_____
Drinking and driving	_____	_____
Texting and driving	_____	_____
Getting a speeding ticket	_____	_____
Alcohol use	_____	_____
Drug use	_____	_____
Setting sexual limits	_____	_____
Danger Zone	_____	_____
Communication	_____	_____
Asset building	_____	_____

_____
Date   Parents signatures   Teen signature

Fair Use: Copies of this activity may be made for personal use. No mass production for distribution, or alteration of this activity is permitted without prior consent of the author.

Interactive Activity #12

Pre-Teen and Parent Contract to Live Well and Experience Healthy Relationships

Pre-Teen: Discuss with your parents and agree on five major decisions you need to make now and stay committed to in order for you to live a happy, healthy and successful life.

Discuss and agree on five major decisions you need to make now and stay committed to so that you will experience healthy relationships as a pre-teen and throughout your life.

Big Life Decisions:

1. _____
2. _____
3. _____
4. _____
5. _____

Decisions Regarding My Teen Relationships:

1. _____
2. _____
3. _____
4. _____
5. _____

_____

Pre-teen Signature   Parent(s) /Guardian(s) Signatures   Date

Fair Use: Copies of this activity may be made for personal use. No mass production for distribution, or alteration of this activity is permitted without prior consent of the author.

"READINGS FOR PARENTS"

*To Help
You Understand
The Importance
Of
Your Parenting Role!*

I Loved You Enough...

Some day when my children are old enough to understand the logic that motivates a parent, I will tell them:

I loved you enough...to ask where you were going, with whom, and what time you would be home.
I loved you enough...to insist that you save your money and buy a bike for yourself even though we could afford to buy one for you.
I loved you enough...to be silent and let you discover that your new best friend was a creep.
I loved you enough...to make you take a Milky Way back to the drugstore (with a bite out of it) and tell the clerk, "I stole this yesterday and I want to pay for it."
I loved you enough...to stand over you for two hours while you cleaned your room, a job that would have taken me ten minutes.
I loved you enough...to let you assume the responsibility for your actions even when the penalties were so harsh they almost broke my heart.
But most of all,
I loved you enough...to say, "NO" when I know you would hate me for it. Those were the most difficult battles of all. I'm glad I won them, because in the end you won something, too.

Erma Bombeck

Dear Parents,

You may not think we are old enough to know about sexuality issues but we are exposed to them much earlier than you can imagine-- long before you think about talking to us about them. We get all kinds of "information" about relationships and sexuality from TV, movies, commercials, music, magazines and friends that are really confusing. This confusion creates tremendous pressure in our already demanding lives. Who/What do we believe -- and who do we go to for help in making the right decisions about these issues? _____?

The answer should be **YOU**, our parents. We know your concerned about decisions that affect our future. It only seems right that **YOU** talk to us and share your values and concerns regarding our relationships and our sexuality.

While it may be difficult/embarrassing for you (and us) to talk about these issues, we really need and want to. It will certainly be easier to deal with awkward feelings together, in a safe environment, before having to deal with them personally, on our own.

(Over) →

© University of Wisconsin Board of Regents

It may seem that we don't listen and value what you have to say but when you are open with us and answer our questions honestly, you really make us think!!! <u>We also need and want to have you listen to our point of view!!!</u>

Remember -- we learn about sexuality issues even if you don't talk with us about them. We want to learn about those issues straight from you -- our parents -- people who care about us and our future

Love, ♡♡

Your Teens

Written by students in Dorothy Wickman's relationships classes at Southern Door County High School, Brussels, Wisconsin.

This letter is written to parents from children in hopes that better communication can be developed. Read it and enjoy!

AS I GROW

Please...

- *Understand that I am growing up and changing very fast. It must be difficult to keep pace with me, but please try.*
- *Listen to me and give me brief, clear answers to my questions. Then I will keep sharing my thoughts and feelings.*
- *Reward me for telling the truth. Then I am not frightened into lying.*
- *Tell me when you make mistakes and what you learned from them. Then I can accept that I am OK, even when I blunder.*
- *Pay attention to me, and spend time with me. Then I can believe that I am important and worthwhile.*
- *Do things you want me to do. Then I have a good, positive model.*
- *Trust and respect me. Even though I am smaller than you, I have feelings and needs just like you.*
- *Compliment and appreciate me. Then I'll feel good, and I'll want to continue to please you.*
- *Help me explore my unique interests, talents, and potential. In order for me to be happy, I need to be me, and not you or someone you want me to be.*
- *Be an individual and create your own happiness. Then you can teach me the same, and I can live a happy, successful and fulfilling life.*
- *Thank you for hearing me; I love you.*

"Excerpt from the book *Successful Parenting*

Fair Use: Copies of this activity may be made for personal use. No mass production for distribution, or alteration of this activity is permitted without prior consent of the author.

Made in the USA
Middletown, DE
22 February 2016